Gourmet Cooking by Earl Peyroux

VOLUME TWO

D1501149

GOURMET COOKING

Learn and enjoy the culinary skills of Paris cooking school graduate, Chef Earl Peyroux.

wsre·tv 23 PBS

A SERVICE OF PENSACOLA JR. COLLEGE

Note on recipes: All recipes in this book and in volume I are intended to prepare for six to eight persons unless otherwise mentioned.

Printed in Pensacola, Florida by the Royal Printing Company

COPYRIGHT © EARL PEYROUX 1985
ALL RIGHTS RESERVED
(REPRINT MAY 1986)

CONTENTS

FOREWORD

Welcome to another of Earl's cookbooks - one, I might add, that you will enjoy reading as much as using. This one has been eagerly awaited since the first was published in 1982.

Earl Peyroux is one of those wonderful people who grew up in New Orleans, a city where one spends life eating, drinking and talking politics. Politics, needless to say, was not Earl's forte. But, much to the pleasure of others, food was.

Earl spent the years of required apprenticeship - at his mother and grandmother's side - before winging it on his own. He studied at the world-famous Cordon Bleu culinary school in Paris. And he has studied with the best of the food world - among them Paul Prudhomme of New Orleans and Nathalie Dupree of Atlanta.

Earl's cooking is influenced heavily by living in the South, with its large variety of fresh produce, and along the Gulf Coast, with its bounty of seafood. It is a well-seasoned, precisely spiced melange of meats, seafood and vegetables. The dishes are never dull and it is a teaser to the eye, tongue and palate. Little coaxing is needed to get up from the chair and head for the kitchen with his book.

Once in Pensacola, he took to the air with the local Public Braodcasting System station producing his "Gourmet Cooking." That show now has more than 160 weeks of taping.

It's from his show that one thing has become apparent. Earl has that rare quality shared by the best food lovers around: He posesses an extraordinary knowledge of his craft and has the rare ability to share his knowledge.

That's the true pleasure of Earl's cookbooks. As a fan of his programs and the first cookbook derived from them, I found it easy to follow his meticulous and concise directions.

The result has been many pleasurable, special moments spent with friends over meals planned and carried out with Earl's cookbook.

This second book is going to be greeted, I am sure, with the same result.

Earl would say bon appetit, or try and enjoy.

I'm telling you: Laissez le bon temps roulee (Let the good times roll.)

Lou Elliott
Journalist
Pensacola News Journal
Pensacola, Florida

INTRODUCTION

In 1982, after six years of producing over one hundred Gourmet cooking shows, we at WSRE-23 were informed that SECA (Southern Eductional Communications Association), the regional network, had decided to make available to all PBS stations throughout the country, fifty-two segments of Gourmet Cooking. We were all elated that our show was deemed worthy to be presented nationally.

Locally in Pensacola, the morning edition of the Pensacola New Journal carried as a regular feature in the food section each week a column which gave the recipes for the upcomming show and WSRE honored requests for recipies by mail and phone. Suddenly we became aware that newspapers in other cities and the PBS stations would not have this information available and we realized we could not satisfy every request on an individual basis. Obviously now was the time to produce a cookbook.

I had been dreaming and working on publishing a book for several years but had not yet had the incentive to bring it to fruition. Now we had one. I immediately sought the clerical, artistic and technical help I needed. We worked constantly for months organizing the data I have been working on for years. We completed the book just as the national broadcast aired. The shows began to air in October 1982 with about eight stations picking us up, Provo, UT having been the first to commit to broadcasting. We began to receive requests for copies of the book and to pick up more and more stations. Mailings began in late November 1982 and as the year 1983 progressed we began to add more and more stations until we reached a peak of fifty-five.

In the summer of 1983, SECA informed us they would carry us another year and wanted fifty-two more shows. Since the book covered 143 shows it corresponded with the shows in 1983 and 1984. When SECA requested another fifty-two for a third year we realized we had a problem. Volume I would cover the shows through mid January 1985 but shows after that would not be in volume I. Back to the drawing board for volume II. Needless to say we are delighted for our third year of acceptance of Gourmet Cooking and the many compliments we receive through the mail.

For the benifit of those who do not have volume I, I am reprinting the Introduction to that volume on the following pages. For those who do have volume I please have another scotch for me and skip the next two pages. For those of you who do not have volume I and would like to, it is available from the above address or you can use the order form at the rear of this book.

In volume I, I acknowledged the help, assistance and encouragement of all those who made the book possible. I wish to acknowledge them once again, however, the foremost acknowledgement for volume II has to be you, the viewers of Gourmet Cooking who have accepted my humble endevors and faults (using the word lovely repeatedly among others) and remained devoted viewers. It is your continued interest that has caused stations to continue broadcasting the show. If you like the show let your station know. They will appreciate it and so will I.

Many thanks to those of you who took the time to write and express your opinion of the show. We gratefully appreciate the compliments as well as the criticisms. God bless you all.

a Bientot

Earl Peyroux

INTRODUCTION

VOLUME I

There are literally thousands of cookbooks on the market today covering every conceivable subject and style of cooking.   Why then, would I presume to write a book about food and its preparation?   To answer that question I must start at the beginning.

Having been reared and having lived for thirty eight years in the city of New Orleans, I was exposed at an early age to a unique and magnificent style of cuisine peculiar to south Louisiana.   At home, my mother, always great in the kitchen, prepared gumbos, bisques, stews, soups and foods typical of our French heritage.   In the homes of relatives and friends, red beans and rice, veal in the French manner, jambalyas, plantins and crepes were served routinely.   In a city renouned for great restaurants, I had a field day with Shrimp Remoulade, Oysters Rockerfeller, Oysters Bienville, Chicken Clemenceau and Bananas Foster.   My interest, however, was as a consumer, and consume I did with enthusiam.   The preparation of food was only of academic interest to me.

It was during my days living in the famed French Quarter of New Orleans that my interest in the prepartation of food began.   At a party given by friends, I was "waxing eloquent" on well known dishes and how they were prepared.   Whereupon, I was instantly challanged by my audience to prepare a feast the coming weekend and share these gourmet delights.   With the bravado that only the third martini can supply, I accepted the challenge, It was only the next day that I realized to what I had committed myself.   I immediately swore off martinis.

When the initial shock of what I had done subsided, I began to prepare for the day of reckoning. Phone calls to relatives and friends supplied recipes, instructions and ideas.   Armed with this information, I prepared a menu and proceeded to shop for the "fixings."   As I proceeded with the preparations my enthusiam began to grow.   Finally, I was equipped with all the ingredients, many recipes, a bottle of scotch, some soda and the Metropolitan Opera broadcast of "La Traviata" to inspire my opus.   I proceeded throught the day chopping onions mincing parsley, sipping scotch, washing lettuce and sipping scotch in what seemed to me a most professional manner.

Frequent visits from my challengers to spur me on and to share my scotch added to the excitement.   The chopping, stuffing and sipping continued until the time for all to gather.   My confidence bolstered by the scotch, was strenthened with the knowledge that cocktails were in order before dinner and would condition the mood of my guests.

At the appointed hour my challengers arrived.   After cocktails we began our feast with a first course of Oysters Rockerfeller served with a good Sauvignon Blanc.   From the buffet my guests served themselves portions of Flank Steak stuffed with oyster dressing, Baked Militon with Shrimp, Cauliflower au Gratin, Tossed Green Salad with Vianigrette Dressing and mounds of hot French bread.   This was accompanied by a beautiful Beaujolais.   The "Oh's" and "Ah's" were all I needed to establish the joys and satisfaction I received from cooking. I had a ball.   Since that day I have needed no special encouragement to execute a meal or for a cocktail party.

In 1963 I got "sand in my shoes" while visiting friends and the beaches and moved to Pensacola, the City of Five Flags.   Pensacola, like New Orleans, has a French and Spanish heritage.   The cooking styles have some similarities but Pensacola has a strong "Southern" influence, flavored with an abundance of seafood from the Gulf of Mexico.

Some years ago, Ann Collins, food editor of the Pensacoa New Journal, featured me and some of my recipes in the food section of the Journal.   Another article by Ann a year or so later prompted Pat Lloyd, fashion editor of the News Journal and longtime personal friend, to recommend me to Dr. Peggy Morrison, head of the home economics department at Pensacola Junior College, as an instructor for a course called "Gourmet Foods".   For two semesters I taught and learned from my students.   What fun we had.

In the meantime, I decided to expand my knowledge of food and its preparation and enrolled in the famous "Le Cordon Bleu Cooking School" in Paris, France. There I spent a glorious six weeks in the capital of good food, learning from the masters. I shared cooking instructions with other students from the USA, England, Japan, Holland, Mexico, Arabia, Canada and Germany. It was an experience I relive daily.

Upon my return from "Le Cordon Bleu", Dr. Morrison suggested a television series on PBS Channel 23 sponsored by the home economics department of the Junior College. The challenge seemed very exciting and the opportunity to discuss food and share what I had learned was tremendous. Peggy arranged a meeting with Bill Farrington, producer and Mike Chamberlain, director at Channel 23 and the TV series "Gourmet Cooking" was launched. Between April and July 1977 we taped thirteen shows and waited for the fall schedule. In October we went on the air and held our breath. The requests for recipes started to come in. We had an audience! In December we started taping again and have continued ever since. As of this writing we have completed one hundred and forty three shows and are continuing to tape new ones.

I have acquired a respectable library of recipes and am constantly requested to share them with friends and acquaintances. The TV exposure has increased the requests for recipes and I have been encouraged by close friends to publish some of them. It has been this encouragement that has prompted me to submit this compilation containing many reipes gathered over the years from family and friends and the Cordon Bleu. The recipes for the one hundred and forty-three shows are included and are indexed in the TV index.

My thanks go back over the years to the original challengers for encouraging me in this interest and for sharing my scotch, and the many New Orleans friends too numerous to mention. Thanks too to many Pensacola friends for sharing many delightful meals and recipes.

Special thanks go to Jerry Gillmore who encouraged me in this cooking experience an has kept me supplied with table flowers for the show, to Howard Meacham, who designed the cover of this book and to David Richbourg, fellow cooking teacher at the Kitchen Shoppe in Pensacola and owner of Dabo's Fine Foods, a gourmet grocery and take out catering service, for assistance and encouragement in the production of this book.

My most specal thanks go to Alma and John, my mother and father. My mother, for so many lessons taught about food preparation and to John who in recent years has discovered the pleasures of cooking New Orleans style and has earned the self-imposed title of H.A.C - half accomplished cook.

It is my sincere wish that all who come into possession of this book will enjoy and use the recipes herein and if they approve of my simple efforts, please have a scotch for me.

Earl Peyroux

Stocks and Sauces

Stocks and Sauces

BOUILLIONS ET FUMETS
STOCKS

BOUILLION DE BOEUF OU VOLAILLE
BEEF OR CHICKEN STOCK

FUMET DE POISSON
FISH STOCK

BOUILLIONS ET FUMETS CREOLE
CREOLE STOCKS

FUMET DE CREVETTES OU ECREVISSE
SHRIMP OR CRAWFISH STOCK

SAUCE BECHAMEL
BASIC WHITE SAUCE

SAUCE CITRON AUX CAPRES
LEMON CAPER SAUCE

SAUCE VELOUTE
WHITE STOCK SAUCE

SAUCE CHARCUTIERE
BUTCHER STYLE SAUCE

SAUCE DIABLE
DEVIL SAUCE

SAUCE AU CITRON
      LEMON VELOUTE SAUCE

SAUCE DEMI-GLACE
      BEEF FLAVORED SAUCE

SAUCE HOLLANDAISE
      HOLLANDAISE SAUCE

SAUCE TOMATE
      TOMATO SAUCE

SAUCE TOMATE
      TOMATO SAUCE

SAUCE BOLOGNAISE
      TOMATO MEAT SAUCE

MAYONNISE
      EGG AND OIL SAUCE

SAUCE VINAIGRETTE
      OIL AND VINEGAR SAUCE

MARINADE POUR VIANDES
      MARINADE FOR MEATS

Stocks and Sauces

The foundation of many sauces is a good stock. This is nothing more than flavor extracted from beef, veal, poultry and vegetables by boiling them in a liquid. Usually water is the basic liquid, however wine is sometimes used to add a little more dimension. Whenever a recipe calls for the addition of water I always ask myself if the flavor of the dish can be enhanced if I use a flavored stock. The following are the basic stocks used in this book.

BOUILLIONS ET FUMETS
STOCKS

While beef or chicken stock is not difficult to make from scratch it is time consuming and frequently the ingredients are not always on hand. For a complete discussion on making stock from scratch I refer the reader to 'Mastering the Art of French Cooking' by Julia Child and 'La Methode' by Jacques Pepin. For a shorter method and for purposes of this book I suggest the following which produces excellent results.

BOUILLION DE BOEUF OU VOLAILLE
BEEF OR CHICKEN STOCK

2	cans	Beef or chicken broth, double strength
2	cans	Water
2	ribs	Celery
2	lg	Carrots
1	lg	Onion
1		Bay leaf
3	stems	Parsley
		Salt and pepper

-Cut all the vegetables into pieces.
-Combine the broth and vegetables in a saucepan.
-Simmer for 30 to 45 minutes.
-Strain.

NOTE: Canned broths tend to be very salty, therefore, add salt only after tasting the broth.

Whenever I have chicken parts - backs, necks, etc. - I usually use them to make my chicken stock rather than throw them away. I simply use them in the above recipe instead of the canned broth, increase the water to cover the other ingredients and follow the directions as stated.

FUMET DE POISSON

FISH STOCK

Fish stock is easy to make and if one obtains the fish bones when purchasing the fish, the ingredients are available.

2	lbs	Fish bones and parts	-Chop all vegetables fine.
1	lg	Onion	-Combine all ingredients in a large saucepan.
2	ribs	Celery	-Bring to a boil.
2	lg	Carrots	-Simmer 45 minutes.
2	cups	Water	-Strain through a fine mesh strainer or
2	cups	White wine	cheesecloth.
1		Bay leaf	
3	stems	Parsley	

If fish bones and parts are not available, substitute for the fish, 2 cups of bottled clam juice. In a pinch the clam juice can be used in place of the fish stock.

BOUILLIONS ET FUMETS CREOLE

CREOLE STOCKS

The frugality of creole and cajun cooking demands that nothing of value be discarded, thus any scraps or so called waste is used if at all possible. Vegetable peelings or scraps, the shells and heads and bones of shrimp, crawfish, or fish, the juices of oysters, bones and scraps of animals are all used to extract the last bit of flavor to be used in the main recipe. Ususally these ingredients are used to make stocks and whenever a recipe calls for the addition of water, the creole or cajun cook will substitute an appropriate stock to heighten the flavor level of the dish such as gumbos, chowders or crawfish or shrimp etoufee.

FUMET DE CREVETTES OU ECREVISSE

SHRIMP OR CRAWFISH STOCK

		Heads and shells of shrimp or crawfish
1	lg	Onion, chopped
1/2	cup	Celery tops
		Salt and pepper
4	cups	water

-Combine heads and shells with onions, celery tops, salt, pepper and water in a stock pot.
-Bring to a boil.
-Simmer about 20 to 30 minutes.
-Strain.

ROUX

In Volume I we discuss in detail the making of a roux and its importance in French and Creole cooking. A roux is the cooking of a quantity of flour in a fat to prepare it to absorb a liquid. Light rouxs are the basis of a Bechamel and a Veloute while dark rouxs are the foundation of gumbos, stews and etoufee.

In French cuisine there are seven basic mother sauces. Master them and you have only to vary them to produce hundreds of others. Volume I covers this thouroughly; however, we will list them here:

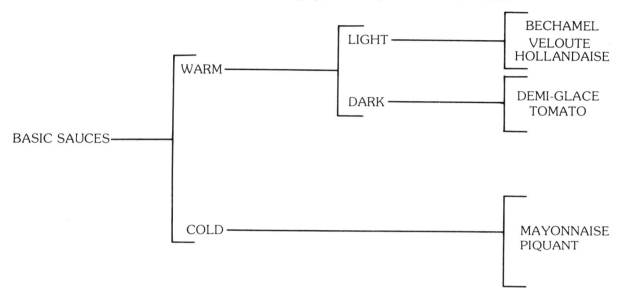

BASIC SAUCES

WARM
- LIGHT — BECHAMEL, VELOUTE, HOLLANDAISE
- DARK — DEMI-GLACE, TOMATO

COLD — MAYONNAISE, PIQUANT

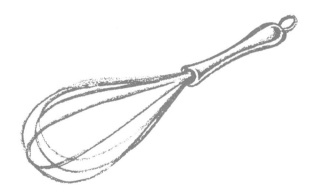

BECHAMEL SAUCE

The most familiar of the mother sauces is Sauce Bechamel, often referred to as a basic white sauce. Flour and fat are cooked together making a basic roux and milk is added. With this base, the variations are many, as illustrated in the following recipes.

SAUCE BECHAMEL

BASIC WHITE SAUCE

4	tbs	Butter	-Melt butter in a heavy bottomed saucepan.
4	tbs	Flour	-Stir in flour and cook for about 1 or 2
2	cups	Milk	minutes.
1/4	tsp	Salt	-Add milk gradually, stirring constantly.
1/8	tsp	White pepper	-Cook until smooth and thick.
			-Add salt and pepper.

If bechamel sauce is to be used as a sauce itself, add the following. Otherwise, proceed with one of its variations.

1/8	tsp	Nutmeg	-Cook slowly until desired consistency.

SAUCE CITRON AUX CAPRES

LEMON CAPER SAUCE

Especially good on salmon croquettes and other fish dishes.

4	tbs	Butter	-Melt butter in a saucepan.
4	tbs	Flour	-Add flour and cook for 2 minutes.
1 1/2	cup	Milk	-Add milk while wisking.
1/3	cup	Lemon Juice	-Cook until thickened.
1/3	cup	Capers	-Add lemon juice, capers, salt and pepper.
		Salt and pepper	-Serve as a garnish to salmon croquettes or other fish dishes.

To extract the maximum juice from lemons or other citrus place them in boiling water and remove from heat for five minutes.

VELOUTE SAUCE

One change in the ingredients for a bechamel sauce and 'voila' you have a veloute sauce. Instead of using milk as the basic liquid in the recipe, stock made from chicken, veal or fish is used. Obviously, the specific dish the sauce will compliment will dictate the use of chicken, veal or fish as the basic flavor of the sauce.

SAUCE VELOUTE

WHITE STOCK SAUCE

Basic stock sauce.

2	tbs	Butter	-Melt butter in a heavy bottomed saucepan.
2	tbs	Flour	-Add flour and stir with wire wisk.
2	cups	Stock (chicken, veal or fish)	-Add stock gradually.
1/2	tsp	Salt	-Stir until thickened.
1/8	tsp	White pepper	-Add salt and pepper.

If veloute sauce is to be used as a sauce itself, add the following. Otherwise, proceed with one of its variations.

| 2 | | Egg yolks | -Add egg yolks and cream. |
| 3 | tbs | Heavy cream | -Blend well. |

SAUCE AU CITRON

LEMON VELOUTE SAUCE

This sauce accompanies any grilled food.

3		Lemons	-Squeeze the juice from 2 lemons.
		Zest of one lemon	-Slice the third in rounds.
3	tbs	Butter	-Melt butter in a skillet.
1	sm	Onion, chopped	-Saute onions.
2	tbs	Flour	-Add the flour and cook 1 minute.
1	cup	White wine	-Pour in the wine, lemon zest and bring to a boil.
3	drops	Tabasco sauce	
1	pinch	Chili powder	-Add the lemon slices, a few dashes of Tabasco, the chili powder and the sugar.
1	tsp	Sugar	
		Salt and pepper	-Salt and pepper to taste.
1	tbs	Parsley	-Cook 5 minutes.
			-Pour into a serving bowl.
			-Sprinkle with parsley.

SAUCE CHARCUTIERE

BUTCHER STYLE SAUCE

A white wine sauce useful for all sorts of pork - grilled, sauteed and roasted. If there are any natural juices when roasting, add them to the sauce.

2		Onions, chopped
4	tbs	Butter
4	tbs	Flour
1 1/4	cup	White wine
1	cup	Chicken stock
1/2	tsp	Dijon mustard
6	sm	Pickles, sweet, chopped
		Salt and pepper

-Heat the wine and stock in a saucepan.
-Saute onions in the butter about 5 minutes on medium heat.
-Add flour to onions and mix well.
-Cook about 2 or 3 minutes.
-Add the wine/stock mixture gradually while stirring.
-Cook on a low heat about 15 minutes stirring from time to time.
-Add the mustard, pickles and parsley.

SAUCE DIABLE

DEVIL SAUCE

A very flavorful sauce used to accompany roast chicken, barbecue and grilled meats.

6		Green onions, chopped
1 1/2	cups	White wine
6	tbs	Vinegar
1/2	tsp	Thyme
1		Bay leaf
6	tbs	Butter
1/3	cup	Flour
1/2	cup	Beef stock
1	tsp	Tomato paste
		Salt and cayenne pepper
1	tbs	Parsley, chopped

-Place onions, wine and vinegar in a saucepan.
-Add thyme and bay leaf.
-Cook until reduced by half.
-Cook the flour in the butter for 2 minutes.
-Add the beef stock and tomato paste.
-Cook for about 10 minutes.
-Add the onion reduction.
-Cook for 3 minutes.
-Season with salt and pepper.
-Strain the sauce.
-Garnish with parsley.

DEMI-GLACE SAUCE

This reduction of aromatic vegetables in an enriched beef stock becomes a mother sauce known as demi-grace. In this base various additions can be made to create other dark warm sauces, such as red wine — Sauce Bordilaise or aromatic vegetables, ham mushrooms and red wine — Marchand de Vin Sauce.

SAUCE DEMI-GLACE

BEEF FLAVORED SAUCE

Basic brown sauce.

1	cup	Onion, chopped
3		Carrots, chopped
3/4	cup	Celery, chopped
4	tbs	Butter
4	tbs	Flour
1	tbs	Beef extract
2	tbs	Tomato paste
2 1/2	cups	Beef stock
1/2	tsp	Thyme
2		Bay leaves
1/2	cup	Parsley, chopped
		Salt and pepper to taste

-Saute onions, carrots and celery in butter for three minutes.
-Add flour and cook slowly to make a dark roux.
-Add beef extract and tomato paste.
-Add beef stock and stir well.
-Simmer for three minutes.
-Add thyme, bay leaves and parsley.
-Add mushrooms and sherry.
-Add salt and pepper.
-Simmer slowly uncovered about 1 hour or until reduced by one third.
-Strain sauce.

OPTIONAL:

1/4	cup	Mushrooms, chopped
1/3	cup	Sherry or madeira

To keep leftover tomato paste, spoon 1 tablespoon (or teaspoon if you prefer) onto a cookie sheet. Freeze well. Store in a plastic bag in refrigerator.

HOLLANDAISE SAUCE

The suspension of butter in egg yolk and lemon is known as Hollandaise, one of the warm light mother sauces. It is easy to make, just remember not to let the mixture boil or the egg will scramble. Like the other mother sauces it has many variations. One such variation is the Sauce Bearnaise below.

SAUCE HOLLANDAISE

HOLLANDAISE SAUCE

Basic butter and egg sauce.

1		Lemon, juice only
4		Egg yolks, beaten
1/2	lb	Butter
1/2	tsp	Salt
	dash	Cayenne

-Add lemon juice to egg yolks in a saucepan.
-Cut butter into fourths.
-Add one part butter to egg.
-Stir constantly with wire wisk.
-When butter completely blends with egg, add more butter.
-Repeat until all butter is smoothly blended wih egg.
-Stir and cook until sauce is thick.
-Remove from heat.
-Add salt and cayenne.
-Beat with wire wisk until smooth - 1/2 minute.
-Pour into another container. The residual heat in the saucepan will cause the sauce to separate.

SAUCE BEARNAISE

TARRAGON FLAVORED HOLLANDAISE

For meat, fish and vegetables.

2	tbs	Tarragon vinegar
1	tbs	Parsley, chopped
1	tsp	Green onion, chopped
3	tbs	Heavy cream

-In a heavy sauce pan blend vinegar, parsley, tarragon and onion.
-Boil rapidly until reduced to one tablespoon.
-Proceed as with the hollandaise.
-Blend in heavy cream.

TOMATO SAUCE

The other mother sauce of the warm dark sauces is tomato sauce and is a blending of herbs, spices and seasonings with tomatoes. The slow simmering for a long time brings about an exquisite blending of flavors and removes the acid taste an undercooked tomato sauce imparts.

SAUCE TOMATE

TOMATO SAUCE

1		Onion, chopped
1		Carrot, chopped
1	rib	Celery, chopped
2	oz	Butter
3	tbs	Flour
1	cup	Stock
4	cups	Tomatoes, diced
2	tsp	Salt
1/8	tsp	Pepper
1	tbs	Sugar
2	tsp	Parsley
2		Bay leaves

-Saute onions, carrots and celery in butter until well done.
-Add flour and cook 3 minutes.
-Add stock, tomatoes, salt, pepper, sugar, parsley and bay leaf.
-Simmer for at least two hours.
-Strain or pass through a food mill.

SAUCE TOMATE

TOMATO SAUCE

Serve with stuffed cabbage or other vegetable dishes which require a tomato sauce.

1		Onion, chopped
3		Tomatoes, peeled and seeded
1/4	tsp	Thyme
		Salt and pepper
16	oz	Tomato sauce

-Saute onions in a little oil.
-Chop tomatoes and add to onions.
-Season with thyme, salt and pepper.
-Add tomato sauce.
-Simmer 15 to 20 minutes.

SAUCE BOLOGNAISE

TOMATO MEAT SAUCE

This sauce is excellent on pasta of all kinds especially ravioli. It is good on rice also.

1/2	lb	Beef, ground
1/2	cup	Bacon, chopped
2		Onions, chopped
4	lg	Tomatoes, peeled and diced
1/8	tsp	Nutmeg, ground
		Salt and pepper
2	tbs	White wine
2	cups	Beef stock

-Saute the beef, bacon and onions in the
     butter until well done.
-Add the tomatoes.
-Season with nutmeg, salt and pepper.
-Cook about 10 minutes.
-Add the wine and stock.
-Cover and simmer for one hour.
-Stir from time to time.

To peel a tomato, turn it over a gas flame with a fork in the stem end or place in boiling water for 30 seconds to one minute. Refresh in cold water for one minute then pull the skin off with the aid of a knife.

MAYONNAISE SAUCE

Although we most often buy our mayonnaise sauce prepared it is hard to beat that made from scratch. Olive oil is gradually incorporated into egg yolk and vinegar to create this cold mother sauce. Add chopped dill pickle, garlic and parsley and 'voila' you have created Tartar Sauce, one of the many variations of this base sauce.

MAYONNAISE

EGG AND OIL SAUCE

Basic cold sauce.

3		Egg yolks
2	tbs	Vinegar
1/2	tsp	Salt
1/8	tsp	White pepper
1/2	cup	Olive oil
1/2		Lemon, juice only

-Have all ingredients at room temperature.
-Beat egg yolks, vinegar, salt and pepper together with a wire wisk.
-Add oil by drops slowly.
-Sauce will thicken after half of oil has been incorporated.
-Add lemon juice.

One medium sized lemon produces 2 to 3 tablespoons of juice and approximately 2 teaspoons of zest.

PIQUANT SAUCE

The following recipes are for a basic vinaigrette sauce and one variation. The many variations available from this mother sauce are included in the Chapter 'Salads and Their Dressings'.

SAUCE VINAIGRETTE

OIL AND VINEGAR SAUCE

1/3	cup	Wine vinegar
1/2	tsp	Salt
1/8	tsp	Pepper
1/4	tsp	Dry mustard (optional)
2/3	cup	Olive oil

-Blend vinegar, salt, pepper and mustard in a bowl.
-Using a wisk, blend in the olive oil a little at a time.

Lemon juice can be substituted for all or part of the vinegar. Two tablespoons of parsley or tarragon or basil can be added according to taste.

MARINADE POUR VIANDES

MARINADE FOR MEATS

This marinade is particularly good for pork and veal.

4	slices	Orange
4	cups	Cider vinegar
1	tsp	Rosemary leaves
1	tsp	Thyme
		Salt and pepper

-Blend together the orange slices, vinegar, rosemary, thyme, salt and pepper.
-Place the meat in the marinade and add cold water to cover the meat.
-Turn the meat several times.
-Cover and refrigerate for 24 hours.

Hors d'Oeuvres

and

First Courses

HORS D'OEUVRES AND FIRST COURSES

RATATOUILLE FROIDE
COLD EGGPLANT

CAPONATA
ITALIAN EGGPLANT APPETIZER

FEUILLES DE RAISINS FARCIES
STUFFED GRAPE LEAVES

HORS D'OEUVRES AUBERGINES
EGGPLANT APPETIZER

TARAMASALATA
CAVIAR DIP

OIGNONS ET CAROTTES LA GRECQUE
GREEK STYLE ONIONS AND CARROTS

ANTIPASTO
ITALIAN VEGETABLE SALAD

CHAMPIGNONS MARINES
MARINATED MUSHROOMS

CHAMPIGNONS SUR CANAPES
MUSHROOM CANAPES

DOIGTS DES CRABES-SAUCE BORDELAISE
CRAB FINGERS BORDELAISE

PINCES DE CRABES MARINEE
MARINATED CRAB CLAWS

HUITRES MARINES
PICKLED OYSTERS

ANTIPASTO DI MARE
     SEAFOOD COCKTAIL

ASPIC DES FOIES
     LIVER ASPIC

MOUSSE DE FOIES DE VOLAILLE
     CHICKEN LIVER MOUSSE

BOULETTES DE BOEUF A L'AIGRE-DOUCE
     SWEET AND SOUR MEATBALLS

SAUCE AIGRE-DOUCE
     SWEET AND SOUR SAUCE

CANAPES OCCITANE
     TOMATO AND ANCHOVY CANAPES

BRIE EN CROUTE
     BRIE IN A PASTRY CRUST

WON TON FRITS
     FRIED WON TON

LES PRUNEAUX AU LARD
     BACON WRAPPED PRUNES

UN APERTIF EN SURPRISE
     STORYVILLE SURPRISE

SIROP SIMPLE
     SIMPLE SYRUP

ABSINTHE FRAPPE
     ABSINTHE FRAPPE

HORS D'OEUVRES AND FIRST COURSES

In France these type recipes along with many salads are commonly taken as a first course. We here in America generally look upon these as party food or cocktail food, mostly to be eaten with our fingers. We present here some we have succesfully served over the years. There are many more, enough to write a special book, but we leave that to another time.

RATATOUILLE FROIDE

COLD EGGPLANT

A cold version of a classic French vegetable dish.

4		Eggplant
4		Onions
2		Red bell pepper
2		Green bell pepper
2	lbs	Zucchini
2	lbs	Tomato
2	cloves	Garlic
1/2	tsp	Sugar
1 1/3	cup	Olive oil
		Salt

-Cut eggplant into quarters lengthwise then into slices.
-Cut zucchini into slices.
-Cut onions into rings.
-Cut tomatoes into eights.
-Cut bell pepper into julienne strips.
-Heat 1/2 the oil in a skillet.
-Saute eggplant.
-Remove and set aside.
-Saute bell pepper and zucchini.
-Remove and set aside.
-Add rest of oil.
-Saute onions.
-Add tomatoes.
-Crush garlic and add to skillet.
-Add salt and sugar.
-Return the cooked vegatables to the skillet.
-Mix well.
-Cover.
-Cook on slow heat about 1 hour stirring 2 or 3 times.
-Let cool in skillet.
-Transfer to serving dish.

CAPONATA

ITALIAN EGGPLANT APPETIZER

Eggplant sauteed with onions, celery, tomatoes and garlic are seasoned Italian style to create a taste of Italy.

1	lg	Eggplant	-Wash eggplant - Do not peel.
		Salt and Pepper	-Cut into 1 inch cubes.
		Vegetable oil	-Season with salt and pepper.
2	med	Onions, chopped	-Fry in heated oil until tender.
2	cloves	Garlic	-Take out and set aside.
3	stalks	Celery, chopped	-Saute onions in same oil until tender.
1	can (lb)	Italian plum tomatoes	-Add garlic, celery, tomatoes, and olives.
10	lg	Green olives, quartered	-Cook slowly 10 minutes.
3	tbs	Pine nuts	-Add eggplant, pine nuts and capers.
1/4	cup	Capers	-Heat vinegar and stir in sugar.
1/4	cup	Wine vinegar	-Add to vegetable mixture.
2	tbs	Sugar	-Season with salt and pepper.
			-Cook 5 minutes longer.
			-Serve chilled as an appetizer or relish.

FEUILLES DE RAISINS FARCIES

STUFFED GRAPE LEAVES

Grape leaves in brine are available at specialty food stores. It's amazing how many they get into a small jar. A delicious appetizer with a Greek flare.

1	8oz jar	Grape leaves	-Rinse leaves in warm water.
1/4	cup	Olive oil	-Cut stem from leaves.
1		Onion, chopped	-Heat oil in skillet.
1/2	cup	Rice, uncooked	-Add onion and saute.
2	tbs	Pine nuts	-Add rice, pine nuts and saute.
1	cup	Chicken broth	-Stir in broth, parsley, salt, pepper, lemon
1/4	cup	Parsley, chopped	juice, and allspice.
1/2	tsp	Salt	-Cover and simmer 15 minutes.
1/8	tsp	Pepper	-Add currants.
1	tbs	Lemon juice	-Set aside.
1/8	tsp	Allspice	-Place rack in dutch oven.
2	tbs	Currants	-Cover with leaves.
			-Stuff leaves.
			-Stack closely.
			-Place a plate over.
			-Add hot water to cover.
			-Simmer 45-50 minutes.
			-Remove and cool.
			-Garnish with lemon.

HORS D'OEUVRES AUBERGINES

EGGPLANT APPETIZER

Baked eggplant is combined with fresh tomatoes and onions, then marinated in a garlic and parsley vinaigrette for a spicy first course.

1		Eggplant
1		Onion, chopped
2		Tomatoes, diced
2	tbs	Parsley, chopped
2	cloves	Garlic, chopped
1	tsp	Salt
1/2	tsp	Pepper
1/3	cup	Olive oil
4	tbs	Wine vinegar

-Place whole eggplant on a baking dish with
   1/2 inch of water.
-Cut off stem and pierce in several places.
-Bake at 400 degrees for 40 minutes.
-Remove from dish.
-Holding with a paper towel remove skin.
-Cool and dice.
-Add onion, tomatoes, parsley and garlic.
-Add salt, pepper, olive oil and vinegar.
-Toss well.
-Refrigerate for one day.

To make small bread containers for hors d'oeuvres cut rounds from thin slices of bread with a 2 inch cookie cutter. Roll thin between sheets of waxed paper. Brush both sides with butter, press into minature muffin pans. Bake at 350 degrees for 15 minutes.

TARAMASALATA

CAVIAR DIP

An hors d'oeuvre of Greek origin uses sliced crispy vegetables as a base for the caviar mixture.

	4oz	Red caviar
1/4	cup	Water
1	cup	Bread crumbs
1/3	cup	Lemon juice
1/2		Onion, chopped
1	cup	Olive oil

-Blend caviar, water, bread crumbs, lemon
   juice, and onion in the bowl of a food
   processor.
-With motor running slowly add the olive oil.
-Blend until the consistency of mayonnaise.
-Refrigerate.
-Serve with slices of cucumber, zucchini,
   yellow squash, cauliflower, etc.

OIGNONS ET CAROTTES A LA GRECQUE

GREEK STYLE ONIONS AND CARROTS

Carrots and onions simmered in wine and oil flavored with fennel seed makes an unusual appetizer served cold or an excellent vegetable dish served hot.

1	lb	Carrots, julienne
2	lbs	Onions, quartered and separated
1	cup	White wine
1/2	cup	Olive oil
1/2	tsp	Thyme
		Juice of 1 lemon
1/2	tsp	Fennel seed
		Salt and pepper
4		Bay leaves

-Bring carrots, onions, wine and oil to a boil.
-Add thyme, lemon juice, fennel seed, salt, pepper and bay leaves.
-Simmer about 12 minutes.
-Serve hot or cold.

ANTIPASTO

ITALIAN VEGETABLE SALAD

Colorful and crunchy, these marinated vegetables can be served on a bed of shredded lettuce as a dinner salad or as an accompaniment to a hardy sandwich.

2	cups	Cauliflower, separated
1	cup	Green pepper, cut into pieces
1	cup	Carrots, sliced
1	cup	Celery, diced
2	cups	Mushrooms, sliced
1/2	cup	Pimiento, chopped
1/2	cup	Tarragon vinegar
2	cloves	Garlic, crushed
1	tsp	Sugar
1	tbs	Dry mustard
		Salt and pepper
1/2	tsp	Dried tarragon
1	cup	Olive oil

-Blanch cauliflower, green pepper and carrots about 5 minutes.
-Refresh in cold water.
-Mix together the cauliflower, green pepper, carrots, celery, mushrooms and pimiento.
-In a mixing bowl blend the vinegar, garlic, sugar, mustard, salt, pepper and tarragon.
-Wisk in the olive oil slowly.
-Pour over the vegetables.
-Let marinate several hours.

CHAMPIGNONS SUR CANAPES

MUSHROOM CANAPES

Small mushrooms are best for this French appetizer of mushrooms sauteed in a light cream sauce and served on bread croutons.

1 1/2	lbs	Mushrooms
6		Green onions, chopped
6	tbs	Port wine
1/3	cup	Cream
3	oz	Butter
6	slices	Bread, crust removed
3	tbs	Parsley, chopped
		Salt and pepper

-Saute green onions in half the butter.
-Add the mushrooms and let cook 2-3 minutes.
-Add the port, salt and pepper.
-Cook 3 minutes.
-Add the cream.
-Cook 2 more minutes.
-Keep warm.
-Cut bread into triangles.
-Melt butter in skillet.
-Saute bread slices on both sides to make croutons.
-Place croutons on serving plate.
-Cover with mushroom mixture.
-Garnish with parsley.

CHAMPIGNONS MARINES

MARINATED MUSHROOMS

These mushrooms bathed in aromatic vegetables and seasonings improve as they age. Refrigerate for a couple of days rather than the one hour indicated.

1	lb	Mushrooms
2	sm	Carrots, peeled
1	lg	Onion, chopped
2	cloves	Garlic, chopped
2		Bay leaves
6	tbs	White wine
3	tbs	Olive oil
		Salt and pepper
2		Tomatoes, peeled
1	tbs	Parsley, chopped

-Dice carrots.
-Saute the carrots, onion and garlic in the oil for 5 minutes.
-Add the bay leaves, wine, salt and pepper.
-Bring to a boil and cook 1 minute.
-Add the mushrooms.
-Cover and cook 4 to 5 minutes on a slow heat.
-Turn from time to time.
-Cool.
-Refrigerate at least 1 hour.
-Slice tomatoes.
-Arrange tomatoes on a serving dish.
-Place mushrooms over tomatoes.
-Garnish with parsley.

ANTIPASTO DI MARE

SEAFOOD COCKTAIL

This seafood and vegetable mixture is great as a first course or as a luncheon salad main course. It always brings raves.

1/2	lb	Squid, small	-Clean squid.
1	lb	Shrimp, shelled	-Cut into small rings leaving the tentacles whole.
1	cup	Oysters	
1		Carrot, sliced	-In a large stock pot place carrots, celery, onions, bay leaf, salt, peppercorns and squid.
1	stalk	Celery, sliced	
1		Onion, sliced	
1		Bay leaf	-Cover with 2 inches of water.
1	tsp	Salt	-Simmer for 15 minutes.
5		Peppercorns	-Add shrimp and oysters.
1/2	clove	Garlic	-Cook for 5 more minutes.
1/2	cup	Green pepper, diced	-Add green pepper last 2 minutes.
1 1/2	tbs	Parsley, chopped	-Remove seafood mixture reserving the liquid.
2		Green onions, sliced	
1	tbs	Capers	-Add parsley.
6	tbs	Olive oil	-Chill mixture.
		Juice of one lemon	-Simmer mushrooms in white wine for 3 minutes.
1/2	lb	Mushrooms, quartered	
2	tbs	White wine	-Add to seafood mixture.
1/4	tbs	Salt	-Chill.
		Pepper	-Blend olive oil, lemon juice, salt and pepper with Dijon mustard.
1	tbs	Dijon mustard	
1/2	head	Lettuce, shredded	-Line serving platter with lettuce.
			-Arrange seafood mixture over lettuce.
			-Pour vinaigrette over all.
			-Serve.

HUITRES MARINES

PICKLED OYSTERS

My good friend Mrs. Sis Lipson provided me with this unusually delicious recipe for oysters. Make plenty, you will need them.

2	qts	Oysters	-Poach oysters in their own juice until they begin to curl.
1	pint	Vinegar	
1/2	cup	Peppercorns	-Remove, drain and reserve liquid.
6	sm	Red peppers	-Scald peppercorns, peppers, allspice, salt, mace and
1	tbs	Allspice, whole	
1	tbs	Salt	cloves in the vinegar.
2		Mace, whole	-Pour over oysters.
8		Cloves, whole	-Add 1 pt. of reserved oyster liquid.
			-Cover and refrigerate.

DOIGTS DES CRABES-SAUCE BORDELAISE

CRAB FINGERS BORDELAISE

Although a classic Bordelaise sauce is made with Bordeaux wine, this version is New Orleans style where a Bordelaise sauce is a combination of olive oil, garlic and parsley. Easy to prepare and delicious.

1	lb	Crab claws, shelled	-Melt butter in a skillet.
4	tbs	Butter	-Add olive oil.
4	tbs	Olive oil	-Add parsley and garlic.
2	tbs	Parsley, chopped	-Add salt and pepper.
2	tsp	Garlic, chopped	-Toss crab claws in the sauce gently until hot.
		Salt and pepper	-Serve from a chafing dish.

PINCES DE CRABES MARINEE

MARINATED CRAB CLAWS

Another of Sis Lipson's recipes which I have adopted as my own. Crab claws marinated in aromatic spices, herbs, wine and olive oil.

1	lb	Crab claws, shelled	-Arrange crab claws in a shallow bowl.
1/4	cup	Wine vinegar	-Blend together the vinegar, salt, pepper,
		Salt and pepper	oregano and garlic.
1/2	tsp	Oregano	-Wisk in the olive oil gradually.
1/2	tsp	Garlic, minced	-Add parsley, cheese, lemon juice,
3/4	cup	Olive oil	worchestershire and wine.
1/2	cup	Parsley, chopped	-Blend well.
2	tbs	Parmesan cheese	-Pour over crab claws.
1	tbs	Lemon juice	-Cover tightly.
1	tbs	Worchestershire sauce	-Refrigerate 24 hours.
1/3	cup	White wine	

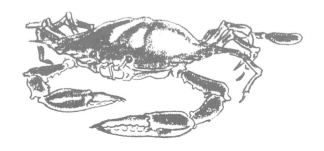

BOULETTES DE BOEUF A L'AIGRE-DOUCE

SWEET AND SOUR MEATBALLS

Tired of Swedish meatballs Try these Chinese style with sweet and sour sauce. They are baked rather than fried.

1		Egg, beaten
1/3	cup	Milk
1/2	cup	Bread cubes
1	tsp	Salt
1/8	tsp	Pepper
1/4	tsp	Sage
1/4	cup	Onions, chopped
1	lb	Ground beef
1	recipe	Sweet and Sour Sauce

-Combine eggs, milk, bread, salt, pepper, sage and onion.
-Blend in the ground beef.
-Shape into small balls.
-Arrange on a rack in a baking pan.
-Bake in a 350 degree oven 15 to 20 minutes until lightly browned.
-Place in a chafing dish.
-Cover with sauce.

SAUCE AIGRE-DOUCE

SWEET AND SOUR SAUCE

1/2	cup	Sugar
1	tbs	Cornstarch
2	tsp	Salt
1/2	cup	Red wine vinegar
1/4	cup	Orange juice
1/4	cup	Pineapple juice
3	oz	Tomato paste

-Blend sugar, cornstarch and salt.
-Stir in vinegar, fruit juices and tomato paste.
-Cook stirring constantly until thickened.

To prevent leftover tomato paste from spoiling pour a little cooking oil over the top and refrigerate.

ASPIC DES FOIES

LIVER ASPIC

A combination of livers, wine, brandy and seasonings is enriched with butter and encased in Port flavored aspic for an outstanding pate.

1	lb	Chicken liver
1	lb	Calf's liver
1/2	oz	Gelatin
1	lb	Butter
1	cup	Port wine
1	tsp	Rosemary
1	tsp	Sage
1	cup	Brandy
		Salt
		Pepper

-Dissolve gelatin in 1/2 cup cold water.
-Bring 1 quart water to a boil.
-Add gelatin.
-Add 1/2 the port wine.
-Cool.
-Chop livers coarsely.
-Saute livers in 2 oz butter with the rosemary
    and sage about 10 minutes.
-Add the rest of the port, salt and pepper.
-Let wine evaporate.
-Put livers through grinder.
-Blend in the rest of the butter and the
    cognac.
-Pour 1/2 the gelatin mixture in a mold.
-Chill.
-Shape pate into a loaf 1/2 inch smaller than
    the mold.
-Place in mold over congeled aspic.
-Pour rest of aspic over pate.
-Chill 2 hours or more.

MOUSSE DE FOIES DE VOLAILLE

CHICKEN LIVER MOUSSE

Serve with lightly toasted French bread slices or crackers of your choice as an accompaniment to cocktails.

1	lb	Chicken livers
2		onions, chopped
2	cloves	Garlic
6	tbs	Cream
3	oz	Butter
3	tbs	Cognac
		Salt and pepper

-Saute the onions and garlic in the butter for 5
    minutes.
-Add the livers and cook for 5 to 6 minutes.
-Add the cognac to deglaze the pan.
-Remove from the heat.
-Add the cream, salt and pepper.
-Puree the mixture in a food processor.
-Pour puree into a mold.
-Refrigerate 1 hour.
-Garnish with lemon slice and chopped
    parsley.

CANAPES OCCITANE

TOMATO AND ANCHOVY CANAPES

Colorful and tasty, these French hors d'oeuvres are a hit when served with cocktails.

6	slices	Bread, thin and with a coarse texture	-Cut bread slices in half.
3	sm	Tomatoes	-Lightly grill in a little butter on both sides.
24		Anchovy fillets, flat	-Mix together half the anchovy fillets, garlic, olive oil and the basil.
5	cloves	Garlic, crushed	-Blend, mashing ingredients to form a creamy sauce.
6	tbs	Olive oil	
1/3	cup	Fresh basil, chopped or	-Spread the grilled bread slices with the sauce.
1	tbs	Dried basil	-Cover with overlapping slices of tomato.
2	oz	Swiss cheese, grated	-Sprinkle with swiss cheese.
12		Black olives, pitted and cut in half	-Run under the broiler for 3 or 4 minutes to melt the cheese.

-Quickly place one anchovy fillet diagonally over tomatoes.
-Place half olive on each side of anchovy.

BRIE EN CROUTE

BRIE IN A PASTRY CRUST

A unique and very French method of serving one of the finest of French cheeses.

1	3-oz	Cream cheese, room temperature	-Blend cream cheese, butter and flour.
1/4	cup	Butter	-Shape into a ball, wrap and refrigerate 1 hour.
3/4	cup	Flour	-Divide dough into 2 parts.
4 1/2	oz	Brie cheese	-Roll each part into a six inch circle, reserving extra dough.
1/2	tsp	Sesame seeds	-Place one circle on an ungreased baking sheet.

-Place the Brie cheese in center.
-Cover with second circle of dough.
-Seal the dough circles together.
-Cut decorative designs from excess dough.
-Garnish croute with cut outs.
-Sprinkle with sesame seeds.
-Bake in a 400 degree oven for 15 to 17 minutes.
-Let stand a few minutes before cutting into small wedges.

LES PRUNEAUX AU LARD

BACON WRAPPED PRUNES

Although this recipe is in volume one of Gourmet Cooking, I repeat it here because it is so good and unusual. Your guests will be asking for the recipe. Nothing could be simpler.

30		Dried prunes, pitted
15	slices	Bacon

-Cut bacon slices in half.
-Wrap each prune in bacon slice.
-Secure with a toothpick.
-Place in a 350 degree oven for 15 to 20
    minutes until bacon is cooked.

WON TON FRITS

FRIED WON TON

These popular chinese appetizers are easy to prepare and can be prepared for frying ahead of time. They go like popcorn so prepare many.

2	tbs	Soy sauce
2	tbs	Sherry
1/4	tsp	Salt
1/4	tsp	Pepper
2	tbs	Peanut oil
1	cup	Pork, finely diced
1	cup	Shrimp, finely diced
2	cups	Bean sprouts
1	cup	Celery, finely diced
1/2	cup	Water chestnuts, diced
1/2	cup	Mushrooms, diced
4		Green onions, chopped
		Won ton wrappers

-Blend soy sauce, sherry, salt and pepper.
-Set aside.
-Heat oil in wok.
-Fry pork and shrimp, stirring, 2 minutes.
-Add green onions, stir-fry 1 minute.
-Add bean sprouts, celery, water chestnuts
    and mushrooms.
-Add reserved sauce.
-Stir-fry 2 minutes.
-Remove from heat.
-Place 1 teaspoon of the mixture into the
    center of
    a won ton wrapper.
-Fold wrapper in half to form a triangle after
    moistening two sides of wrapper.
-Fry until golden in 2 inches of oil.
-Drain.
-Serve with Chinese hot mustard and sweet
    and sour sauce.

ABSINTHE FRAPPE

ABSINTHE FRAPPE

The anise flavor stimulates the appetite. Traditionally served as an aperitif for a New Orleans brunch.

1 1/2	oz	Absinthe or Pernod
2	dashes	Simple syrup
		Soda water

-Fill 8 oz highball glass with crushed ice.
-Add absinthe and syrup.
-Slowly add soda water.
-Stir vigorously until outside of glass becomes frosted.
-(Serves one)

UN APERTIF EN SURPRISE

STORYVILLE SURPRISE

One of two drinks I serve in my New Orleans brunch classes. Storyville was a section of New Orleans in the late ninteenth century where the ladies of the night applied their trade.

1 1/2	oz	Rum
1 1/2	oz	Vodka
1 1/2	oz	Simple syrup
3	oz	Pineapple juice
1/2	tsp	Lemon juice
		Pineapple chunks
		Maraschino cherries

-Pour all liquid ingredients over crushed ice.
-Shake well.
-Garnish with pineapple and cherries.
-(Serves four)

SIROP SIMPLE

SIMPLE SYRUP

1/2	cup	Sugar
1/2	cup	Boiling Water

-Add boiling water to sugar.
-Stir quickly until liquid is clear.
-Cool.

Eggs and Cheese

EGGS AND CHEESE

OEUFS POCHES OSTENDAISE
POACHED EGGS AND SHRIMP IN PASTRY SHELLS

OEUFS POCHES
POACHED EGGS

SAUCE CREVETTES
SHRIMP SAUCE

OEUFS SAINT LOUIS
EGGS SAINT LOUIS

OEUFS A L'ALSACIENNE
EGGS AND SAUERKRAUT GRATINEE

CROUSTADES AUX ANCHOIS
POACHED EGGS IN BREAD CASES WITH ANCHOVY

CROUSTADES
BREAD CASES

CREPES FARCIES FORESTIERE
HAM, EGG AND MUSHROOM CREPES

CREPES
FRENCH PANCAKES

OMELETTE ESPANGNOL
SPANISH OMELET

EGGS AND CHEESE

One of my favorite styles of entertaining in New Orleans was the Sunday Brunch. Sometimes we did a Sunday Brunch on other days of the week but still called it Sunday Brunch. This is a meal composed of traditional breakfast foods combined with lunch recipes served from 11 AM to 1 PM served with bloody Marys or other type drinks. There are many delicious recipes that have been developed for this type entertaining such as Eggs Hussard and Eggs Peyrous (Volume I). Here we present some new ones - Eggs Ostendaise and Eggs Saint Louis Louis as well as others. Try, and enjoy.

OMELETTE ESPANGNOL

SPANISH OMELET

A tasty filling of tomatoes, onions, olives, pimiento, green peas and bell peppers fills these omelets for a bit of Sapin.

2	med	Tomatoes, peeled, seeded and chopped
1		Onion, grated
2	tbs	Butter
6		Olives, stuffed
1/2	cup	Green peas
1	tbs	Pimiento, chopped
1/2	cup	Green peppers, chopped
3		Eggs
2	tbs	water
		Salt and pepper
1	tbs	Butter
1	tbs	Oil

-Saute tomatoes and onions in butter.
-Add olives, green peas, pimiento and green pepper.
-Cook on low heat for 5 minutes.
-Beat eggs, water, salt and pepper until well blended.
-Heat butter and oil until hot in an omelet pan.
-Pour egg mixture into pan.
-Reduce heat to medium.
-When egg becomes slightly firm on top place vegetable mixture on down the center.
-Lift and roll 1/3 of omelet over the vegetables.
-Grab the handle of the pan with palm underneath.
-Gently slide unfolded edge of omelet onto a plate.
-Turn pan over so that the vegetables and folded omelet fall over the 1/3 on the plate.
-Garnish with more sauce if desired.
-This serves two. Do not double recipe. Make twice or three times. First will hold in a 200 degree oven.

OEUFS SAINT LOUIS

EGGS SAINT LOUIS

For a New Orleans style brunch, try these bread boats filled with ham, mushrooms, onions and bell pepper topped with a poached egg. This recipe is named in honor of the patron saint of New Orleans, King Louis IX of France.

4		Brown and serve rolls	-Cut rolls in half and scoop out centers.
1	cup	Mushrooms, sliced	-Brush inside with melted butter.
1 1/2	cup	Ham, diced	-Bake as directed reducing time by 5 minutes.
1	tbs	Butter	-Saute mushrooms and ham in butter.
1	tbs	Flour	-Set aside.
1/3	cup	Bell pepper, chopped	-Cook flour in butter for 2 minutes.
1/2	cup	Onions, chopped	-Add onions and bell pepper.
1/3	cup	Pimiento, chopped	-Cook for 3 - 4 minutes.
1/2	cup	Milk	-Add pimiento.
1/2	cup	Chablis	-Blend in milk and chablis.
		Salt and pepper	-Salt and pepper.
8		Poached eggs	-Add mushrooms and ham.
1/2	cup	Swiss cheese, grated	-Fill bread container 3/4 full with ham mixture.

-Place a poached egg on top.
-Cover with more sauce.
-Sprinkle with swiss cheese.
-Bake in oven or run under broiler until cheese melts.

OEUFS A L'ALSACIENNE

EGGS AND SAUERKRAUT GRATINEE

These six minute eggs - half soft and half hard - are placed on a bed of sauerkraut, garnished with a mornay sauce and browned in the oven for a taste of the northeast region of France.

12		Eggs	-Plunge the eggs in a large pot of boiling water.
4	tbs	Butter	-Cook exactly six minutes.
4	tbs	Flour	-Gently shell the eggs and refresh in cold water.
1	qt	Milk	-Melt butter in a saucepan.
1	lb	Sauerkraut, drained and washed	-Add the flour blending well.
1/4	tsp	Nutmeg, ground	-Add the milk.
		Salt and pepper	-Season with the nutmeg, salt and pepper.
1/4	lb	Swiss cheese, grated	-Bring just to the boil while stirring.

-Spread the sauerkraut in a baking dish.
-Place the eggs over sauerkraut.
-Cover with the sauce.
-Sprinkle with cheese.
-Bake in a 450 degree oven for 10 minutes.

CROUSTADES AUX ANCHOIS

POACHED EGGS IN BREAD CASES WITH ANCHOVY

Toasted bread containers are filled with sauteed eggplant, topped with a poached egg and garnished with anchovy filets. These are then placed on top of fresh tomato sauce.

3	lbs	Tomatoes, cut in quarters
4	cloves	Garlic, chopped
2	lg	Onions, chopped
2	tbs	Oil
		Salt and pepper
1	tbs	Sugar
3	tbs	Olive oil
3	med	Eggplant, peeled and cut into small cubes.
6		Croustades, heated
6		Eggs, poached
12		Anchovy filets
1	tsp	Basil

-Saute the onions in oil with half the garlic for 5 minutes.
-Add the tomatoes.
-Add salt, pepper and sugar.
-Cook for 15 minutes.
-Strain.
-Keep warm.
-Saute the eggplant with the remaining garlic about 10 minutes.
-Salt and pepper.
-Place the croustades on a serving dish or individual plates.
-Fill them three-fourths full with the eggplant.
-Place an egg over the eggplant.
-Arrange two filets of anchovy over egg.
-Pour the sauce around the croustades.
-Sprinkle with basil.

To POACH, which is a form of boiling, means to cook in a liquid which is about 180 degrees where the water is just barely moving but not yet bubbling. Usually used to cook delicate foods such as eggs or fish.

CROUSTADES

BREAD CASES

These toasted bread containers can be filled with a variety of foods but are especially good for poached egg dishes. They can be made well ahead of time and can be frozen.

2	loaves	Bread, firm and course, unsliced
8	tbs	Butter, melted

-Obtain from your baker or bake two loaves of bread.
-Cut crust off all four sides.
-Cut loaf into 1 1/2 inch slices.
-This should yield 4 or 5 cubes of bread about 3 1/2 x 3 1/2 x 1 1/2 inches.
-Cut or scoop out the centers leaving sides of 1/2 inch and 1 inch deep.
-Brush all sides of the bread container with butter.
-Place on a cookie sheet and bake at 300 degrees for 45 minutes.
-Remove from oven and allow to cool.

CREPES FARCIES FORESTIERE

HAM, EGG AND MUSHROOM CREPES

Breakfast in a crepe. Ham, mushrooms and eggs are enclosed in a French pancake, sprinkled with cheese and browned in the oven.

1/2	lb	Boiled ham, diced
1/2	lb	Mushrooms, quartered
4	tbs	Butter
		Salt and pepper
2	tbs	Parsley, chopped
2		Eggs, beaten
1/4	cup	Cream
1/4	cup	Swiss cheese, grated
12		Crepes

-Saute the ham and mushrooms in the butter.
-Add the salt, pepper and parsley.
-Mix all well.
-Blend the eggs and cream together.
-Add to the ham/mushroom mixture.
-Cook until the eggs are firm but soft.
-Place some of the mixture on each crepe.
-Roll the crepes and place on an oven proof dish.
-Sprinkle with cheese.
-Run under the broiler until the cheese is lightly browned.

CREPES

FRENCH PANCAKES

3/4	cup	Flour
1/8	tsp	Salt
1	tbs	Oil
1	cup	Milk
2		Eggs, beaten
2	tbs	Butter

-Blend together the flour, salt, oil and milk.
-Add the eggs.
-Let rest one hour.
-Make 12 crepes using the 2 tablespoons butter.

Chill cheese very cold to facilitate shredding.

OEUFS POCHES OSTENDAISE

POACHED EGGS AND SHRIMP IN PASTRY SHELLS

One of the many special recipes we made at the Cordon Bleu. Crisp pastry shells are filled with shrimp, poached eggs and hollandaise sauce.

12	Baked tartlette shells	-Fill tartlette shell with shrimp sauce.
12	Poached eggs	-Place one poached egg on top.
	Shrimp sauce	-Cover with hollandaise.
	Hollandaise sauce	-Heat under broiler or in oven.
	Chopped parsley	-Garnish with a little parsley.

OEUFS POCHES

POACHED EGGS

2	qts	Water	-Heat water and vinegar to simmering.
1/2	cup	White vinegar	-Drop one egg at a time into water.
12		Eggs	-Spoon water over to shape egg.
			-Cook about 3 minutes until firm outside (white) and liquid inside (yolk).
			-With a slotted spoon remove eggs to a bowl of cool water.
			-To reheat - replace cool water with hot.

SAUCE CREVETTES

SHRIMP SAUCE

2	cups	Milk, warm	-Melt butter in a saucepan.
4	tbs	Butter	-Stir in flour and cook 2 minutes.
1/3	cup	Flour	-Add milk blending well.
1/2	tsp	Salt	-Add salt and pepper.
		Pepper	-Cook until thick.
1/3	cup	Cream	-Add cream and shrimp.
1/2	cup	Cooked shrimp	-Add mushrooms to shrimp sauce.
1/2	cup	Mushrooms, sauteed in butter	-Place in a double boiler until ready.

Hard boiled eggs peel easily if shelled immediately after being refreshed in cold running water. Store in a bowl of water until ready to use.

For greater volume heat egg whites at room temperature. To bring refrigerated eggs to room temperature place eggs in a bowl and cover with hot water from the faucet. Let rest for fifteen minutes.

To keep leftover egg yolks when separating eggs cover them with water in a small bowl and they will keep a few days in the refrigerator.

Salads

and

Their Dressings

SALADS AND THEIR DRESSINGS

SALADE DE POMMES DE TERRE SUISSE
    SWISS POTATO SALAD

POMMES PROVENCALES
    POTATOES PROVENCE STYLE

SALADE BELLE HELENE
    CELERY ROOT SALAD

SALADE DES EPINARDS ET DES TOMATES
    SPINACH AND TOMATO SALAD WITH HORSERADISH CREAM DRESSING

SALADE MELANGEE AUX FROMAGE BLEU
    MIXED SALAD WITH BLUE CHEESE

SALADE AU PERSIL
    PARSLEY SALAD

SALADE DES HARICOTS VERTS
    MARINATED GREEN BEAN SALAD

SALADE AU BROCOLI EN ROND
    BROCCOLI SALAD RING

SALADE AUX BROCOLI
    BROCCOLI SALAD

BROCOLIS NICOIS
    BROCCOLI NICE STYLE

SALADE DE CHOU ROUGE ET ANANAS
    RED CABBAGE AND PINEAPPLE SALAD

SALADE DE CHOU ET POMMES
    CABBAGE AND APPLE SALAD

RATATOUILLE FROID
    COLD EGGPLANT SALAD

SALADE DES MIRLITON
    VEGETABLE PEAR SALAD

SALADE DES COMBOS ET TOMATES
OKRA AND TOMATO SALAD

SALADE TOMATES FARCIE AUX BROCOLIS
TOMATOES STUFFED WITH BROCCOLI SALAD

SALADE DE COURGETTES ET DE CHAMPIGNONS
ZUCCHINI AND MUSHROOM SALAD

SALADE DE BETTERAVES AUX NOIX
BEET AND WALNUT SALAD

SALADE DE CRUDITES
VEGETABLE SALAD

SALADE DE RIZ
RICE SALAD

CELERI AUX POMMES ET AUX NOIX
APPLES AND WALNUT SALAD

AVOCAT AU PAMPLEMOUSSE
AVOCADO AND GRAPEFRUIT SALAD

SALADE DE PAMPLEMOUSSE ET DES CONCOMBRES
GRAPEFRUIT AND CUCUMBER SALAD

SALADE PASTA PRIMAVERA
PASTA PRIMAVERA SALAD

SALADE D'OLIVE ITALIENNE
ITALIAN OLIVE SALAD

SALADE DES HUITRE
OYSTER SALAD

VINAIGRETTE SAUCE
SAUCE VINAIGRETTE

SAUCE CREOLE
CREOLE DRESSING

SAUCE A LA CREME FRANCAISE
CREAM FRENCH DRESSING

SALADS AND THEIR DRESSINGS

Cool, crunchy and refreshing salads usually become an interlude between first course or soups and the main course. Occasionally they are an accompaniment to the main course which is my preference or among many French people it comes after the main course before dessert. Frequently they are the main course for light lunches.

Whatever your preference we present here a group of salads that appeal to the eye as well as to the taste. I hope you will enjoy and try them all.

SALADE DE POMMES DE TERRE SUISSE

SWISS POTATO SALAD

Swiss cheese and knockwurst are added to potatoes for a hardy and tasty salad.

4		Knockwurst
1	cup	Emmenthaler cheese, julienne
3/4	cup	Diced celery
1 1/2	cups	Cooked, sliced potato
1/2	cup	Chopped green onions
2	tbs	Dijon Mustard
1/2	cup	Mayonnaise

-Simmer knockwurst in hot water for 15 minutes.
-Drain, cook, peel and slice.
-Place in a bowl and add Emmenthaler cheese.
-Add celery, potato and green onions.
-Mix together the mustard and mayonnaise.
-Add to salad mixture and blend well.

POMMES PROVENCALES

POTATOES PROVENCE STYLE

This fall salad is unique in that is is baked. Potatoes, onions and tomatoes are seasoned in a casserole and baked. Allowed to cool it is served as a salad.

2	lbs	Potatoes, peeled and sliced in rounds
1		Onion, cut in two, then sliced
1	lb	Tomatoes, sliced
1	can	Anchovy filets
1/2	tsp	Herbs de Provence
2	tbs	Olive oil

-Blend the anchovies and the herbs forming a paste.
-Brush a baking dish with some of the olive oil.
-Place a layer of potatoes in the dish.
-Cover them with half the onions and tomatoes.
-Cover with half the anchovy paste.
-Repeat layers with remaining ingredients.
-Pour Olive oil over layers.
-Bake 1 hour and 15 minutes.
-Allow to cool.

SALADE BELLE HELENE

CELERY ROOT SALAD

A classic French salad uses a vegetable seen more and more in the markets, celery root or celeraic. This was a common vegetable one hundred years ago in American cooking. The root has a concentrated celery flavor and makes a delicious salad.

4	cups	Celery root, cut in julienne
1/2	tsp	Salt
2		Egg yolks, hard cooked and chopped
1		Egg yolk, raw
1	tsp	Wine vinegar
		Salt and white pepper
3/4	cup	Olive oil
1	tsp	Parsley, chopped
6	slices	Cooked beets
6	lg	Black olives
6		Walnut halves

-Blanch celery root in boiling water.
-Refresh in cold water.
-Dry in towels and set aside.
-Place in a bowl the hard cooked and raw egg yolks, the vinegar, salt and pepper.
-Wisk in olive oil until it forms a mayonnaise.
-Fold in the parsley.
-Blend with the celery root.
-Shape into a mound on a serving plate.
-Cut beets into crescents using a fluted pastry cutter.
-Arrange around salad.
-Cut olives in half and place one above each beet crescent.
-Place walnuts in a circle on top.

> **Cook eggs in simmering water, not hard boiling, and the whites will remain tender. High heat toughens the protein and makes them leathery.**

SALADE DES EPINARDS ET DES TOMATES

SPINACH AND TOMATO SALAD WITH HORSERADISH CREAM DRESSING

Tomatoes marinated in a cream vinaigrette are served over a bed of fresh lettuce for a colorful and flavorful salad.

1	lb	Fresh spinach, cleaned
1	tbs	Horseradish
2	tbs	Dijon mustard
1/2	cup	Parsley, chopped
1/2	cup	Green onions, chopped
		Salt and pepper
1/3	cup	White wine vinegar
1	cup	Heavy cream
3		Tomatoes cut into eights
1	cup	Croutons

-Arrange lettuce on a serving platter.
-Blend in a bowl the horseradish, mustard, parsley, onions, salt, pepper and vinegar.
-Wisk in the heavy cream.
-Place tomatoes in dressing.
-Mix well.
-Distribute the tomatoes and dressing over the spinach.

SALADE MELANGEE AUX FROMAGE BLEU

MIXED SALAD WITH BLUE CHEESE

Fresh and crispy salad greens are combined with the tangy taste of blue cheese before the sour cream vinaigrette seasoned with Herbs de Provence is added.

1	sm	lettuce	-Clean lettuce, watercress and spinach.
1	bunch	Watercress	-Break into small pieces.
1	bunch	Spinach	-Place in a salad bowl.
8		Green onions chopped	-Sprinkle green onions over.
6		Eggs, hard cooked	-Place egg slices on top.
6	oz	Blue cheese crumbled	-Sprinkle blue cheese over all.
1/4	cup	White wine vinegar	-Refrigerate.
1/2	cup	Sour cream	-Blend together the vinegar, sour cream,
1/4	tsp	Herbs de Provence	Herbs de Provence, salt and pepper.
		Salt and pepper	-Blend in the Olive oil.
3/4	cup	Olive oil	-At serving time pour dressing over the
2	cups	Croutons	greens.
			-Garnish with croutons.

SALADE AU PERSIL

PARSLEY SALAD

A most unusual salad presented by a cooking school teacher friend, Joe Middleton, during a class. It is delicious and will surprise you.

2		Parsley bunches	-Remove sprigs of parsley from the stems.
2	tbs	Wine vinegar	-Chill sprigs in a covered bowl.
		Salt and pepper	-Combine the vinegar, salt, pepper and olive
6	tbs	Olive oil	oil.
2	cloves	Garlic	-Crush garlic.
3/4	cup	Parmesan cheese	-Add to vinaigrette.
			-Toss parsley with the parmesan cheese.
			-Add vinaigrette.
			-Toss well.
			-Serve immediately.

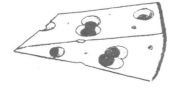

SALADE AU BROCOLI EN ROND

BROCCOLI SALAD RING

Broccoli and red onions are pressed into a ring mold for an attractive presentation of this flavorful vegetable. A seasoned vinaigrette and quartered hard cooked eggs are the garnish.

4	cups	Broccoli, cut small
1	lg	Red Onion, chopped
8		Eggs, hard boiled and quartered
1	recipe	Vinaigrette sauce

-Blanch broccoli in boiling water for five
minutes.
-Chill.
-Spray a ring mold with Pam.
-Place onion in bottom of ring.
-Fill mold with broccoli.
-Press down hard with a spoon or spatula.
-Unmold on a serving dish.
-Arrange egg quarters around and in the
center of mold.
-Pour vinaigrette over.

SALADE AUX BROCOLI

BROCCOLI SALAD

Red onion and chopped hard cooked eggs garnish broccoli flowerettes which is sauced with a Creole vinaigrette dressing.

1	lb	Broccoli, separated into florettes
2		Eggs, hard cooked
1	lg	Red onion
1	recipe	Creole Vinaigrette dressing

-Boil broccoli in salted boiling water until
tender.
-Refresh under cold water.
-Chop hard cooked eggs.
-Cut onion into thin slivers.
-Arrange broccoli on a serving dish.
-Sprinkle with cooked egg.
-Garnish with red onion slivers.
-Pour vinaigrette over all.

Immediately plunge hard cooked eggs into cold running water to prevent the yolks from turning dark.

BROCOLIS NICOIS

BROCCOLI NICE STYLE

The classic Salade Nicoise is modified to make broccoli the main theme while retaining some of the classic ingredients. Colorful and tasty.

1 1/2	lbs	Broccoli
1	cup	Tuna, white, packed in water.
3		Eggs, hard cooked
1	can	Anchovy filets
12		Black olives, pitted
1	cup	Vinaigrette sauce
1	tsp	Dijon mustard

-Remove broccoli flowerettes, peel and slice stems.
-Blanch in boiling water for 5 minutes.
-Refresh in cold water.
-Arrange on a serving platter.
-Cut eggs in quarters and arrange over broccoli.
-Place anchovy filets and olives over broccoli and eggs.
-Add mustard to vinaigrette.

SALADE DES HARICOTS VERTS

MARINATED GREEN BEAN SALAD

This very French salad is especially good when made with very tender and young green beans. They are blanched and refreshed in cold water to set their color. Garnish with a seasoned vinaigrette dressing.

3	cups	Green beans, cut french style
1/3	cup	Pimiento, sliced
1	cup	Red onion, sliced
1	cup	Celery
1/2	cup	Vinegar
1	clove	Garlic, crushed
2	tsp	Paprika
		Salt and pepper
1	cup	Olive oil

-Blanch green beans for five to eight minutes until tender.
-Refresh in cold water.
-Blend together the beans, pimiento, onions and celery.
-Mix together the vinegar, garlic, paprika, salt and pepper.
-Wisk in the olive oil gradually.
-Pour over the vegetable mixture
-Marinate over night.

SALADE DES MIRLITON

VEGETABLE PEAR SALAD

This unusual vegetable so common in South America where it is called a chyote and in the New Orleans area where it is called mirliton was presented in volume one as a hot vegetable dish stuffed with shrimp or crab meat. Here it is served as a salad.

6		Mirlitons
5	tbs	Olive oil
4	tbs	Vinegar
1/2	tsp	Mustard
		Salt and pepper
2	tbs	Parsley, chopped
1/2	tsp	Thyme

-Cut mirlitons in half.
-Boil in salted water until tender, about 30 minutes.
-Drain and refresh in cold water.
-Peel pears and remove seed.
-Slice into bite size pieces.
-Blend together olive oil, vinegar, mustard, salt, pepper and thyme.
-Add parsley.
-Pour over mirlitons.

RATATOUILLE FROID

COLD EGGPLANT SALAD

This is a cold version of the classic Mediterranean dish, ratatouille. Eggplant, zucchini, tomatoes, onions and bell pepper are sauteed then braised slowly in garlic flavored olive oil. Excellent as a salad or as an hors d'oeuvre.

4		Eggplant, cut in pieces
1 1/2	cup	Olive Oil
4		Bell pepper, sliced
2	lbs	Zucchini, sliced
4		Onions, sliced
2	lbs	Tomatoes, cut in eights
2	cloves	Garlic, crushed
		Salt
1/2	tsp	Sugar

-Saute the eggplant in 1/3 the olive oil for about 5 to 8 minutes.
-With a skimmer remove the egglant.
-Saute the bell pepper and zucchini in the same way.
-Remove and set aside.
-Add more oil to skillet.
-Saute the onions for 5 minutes.
-Add the tomatoes.
-Add the crushed garlic.
-Add the sugar and salt.
-Return all the vegetables to the skillet.
-Cover and cook over very low heat about one hour.
-Turn vegetables 2 or 3 times during the cooking.
-Let mixture cool.

SALADE DE COURGETTES ET DE CHAMPIGNONS

ZUCCHINI AND MUSHROOM SALAD

A garlic vinaigrette is the marinade for blanched slices of zucchini and mushrooms for a wonderful salad.

1	lb	Mushrooms, large	-Slice the mushrooms.
3		Zucchini, small	-Marinate in the vinaigrette.
1/2	cup	Vinaigrette sauce	-Cut zucchini into 1/4 inch slices.
		Salt and pepper	-Blanch in boiling water 5 minutes.
1	tbs	Parsley	-Refresh in cold water.
		Lettuce leaves	-Drain well.

-Add to mushrooms and vinaigrette.
-Salt and pepper.
-Marinate 15 minutes.
-Add parsley blending well.
-Serve over lettuce leaves.

SALADE DE CRUDITES

VEGETABLE SALAD

A mixture of green vegetables blanched and refreshed are blended with a mustard vinaigrette and red onion for a crunchy and tasty green salad.

1	lb	Green beans, cut to 2 in lengths	-Blanch beans, zucchini and peppers.
5	sm	Zucchini, cut into 1 in lengths then quartered	-Refresh under cold water. -Blend mustard, vinegar, garlic and pepper.
2		Sweet peppers cut into strips	-Wisk in olive oil.
2	tsp	Dijon Mustard	-Arrange vegetables in a serving dish.
2	tbs	Red wine vinegar	-Sprinkle with onions and basil.
2	cloves	Garlic, minced	-Pour dressing over vegetables.
		Pepper	
1/2	cup	Olive oil	
1/2	cup	Red onion, chopped	
1	tsp	Basil	

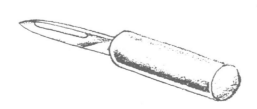

SALADE DE CHOU ET POMMES

CABBAGE AND APPLE SALAD

Blanched and refreshed cabbage is combined with apples and raisins and garnished with a seasoned vinaigrette for a crunchy and fruity salad for fall and winter.

1		Cabbage, shredded	-Blanch cabbage in boiling water for one
3		Apples, diced	minute.
1/3	cup	Raisins	-Drain and refresh.
1/3	cup	Olive oil	-Mix together cabbage, apples and raisins.
2/3	cup	Red wine vinegar	-Blend together the olive oil, vinegar, cumin,
1/2	tsp	Cumin	chevril, sugar, salt and pepper.
1	tsp	Chevril	-Pour over cabbage mixture.
1	tsp	Sugar	-Toss well.
		Salt and pepper	-Refrigerate.

To plump raisins soak them in a small amount of white wine for 20 minutes.

SALADE DE CHOU ROUGE ET ANANAS

RED CABBAGE AND PINEAPPLE SALAD

A colorful and flavorful salad is this combination of shredded red cabbage, pineapple and green onions marinated in a vinaigrette

1/4	cup	Pineapple juice	-Add 1/4 cup pineapple juice to vinegar.
6	cups	Red cabbage, shredded	-Blend together the cabbage, pineapple,
2	cups	Pineapple, diced	onions and raisins.
1	cup	Green onions, chopped	-Pour vinaigrette over vegetables.
6	oz	Raisins	-Chill.
1/2	cup	Vinaigrette	

SALADE DES GOMBOS ET TOMATES

OKRA AND TOMATO SALAD

Quickly blanched and refreshed okra remains crunchy and is blended with diced tomatoes and sauces with a spicy Creole vinaigrette.

1/2	lb	Okra, whole
3	lg	Tomatoes
1/2	cup	Creole dressing

-Blanch okra in boiling water for about 5 to 7 minutes.
-Refresh in cold water.
-Slice okra into 1/2 inch pieces.
-Peel tomatoes.
-Cut tomatoes into 1/2 inch pieces.
-Blend together the okra, tomatoes and the creole dressing.

SALADE TOMATES FARCIES AUX BROCOLIS

TOMATOES STUFFED WITH BROCCOLI SALAD

Attractive and tasty, this salad of hollowed out tomatoes, filled with diced tomato, broccoli and rice, is flavored with a sour cream vinaigrette.

6		Tomatoes
1	cup	Cooked rice
1	cup	Broccoli, blanched and chopped
1/2	tsp	Basil
		Salt and pepper
1/2	cup	Sour cream
2	tbs	Vinegar

-Cut tops off tomatoes.
-Squeeze out seeds.
-Remove pulp and chop.
-Blend together the tomato pulp, broccoli and rice.
-Add basil, salt and pepper.
-Blend in sour cream and vinegar.
-Fill tomato shells.
-Serve on a bed of lettuce.

SALADE DE BETTERAVES AUX NOIX

BEET AND WALNUT SALAD

Beets and walnuts are an unusual combination but when combined with sour cream and horseradish they provide a unique experience.

1/2	cup	Cream
1/2	cup	Sour cream
1	tbs	Horseradish
6	cups	Beets, diced
4	oz	Walnuts, shelled
		Juice of one orange
		Salt and pepper
1	tbs	Chives

-Blend together the cream, sour cream, and
   the horseradish.
-Beat lightly with a wisk.
-Add beets, walnuts and orange juice.
-Blend well.
-Salt and pepper.
-Sprinkle with chives.
-Serve on a bed of lettuce.

CELERI AUX POMMES ET AUX NOIX

APPLES AND WALNUT SALAD

Crisp celery, apples and walnuts are combined with a mustard vinaigrette dressing for an exciting salad.

8	stalks	Celery, diced
6		Apples, red delicious, sliced
1	cup	Walnuts or pecans, chopped
3	tbs	Mustard
6	tbs	Wine vinegar
6	tbs	Olive oil
		Salt and pepper

-Blend the mustard, salt, pepper and vinegar.
-Add oil wisking vigorously.
-Add the celery, apples and nuts.
-Blend well.
-Let rest 15 minutes.

SALADE DE LEGUMES VERTS

GREEN VEGETABLE SALAD

Crisp, crunchy and colorful this mixture of fresh vegetables is dressed with a mustard and garlic vinaigrette dressing.

1	cup	Green peas, blanched
2	cups	Green beans, cut French style and blanched
1	cup	Celery, sliced
1	cup	Green bell pepper, diced
1	cup	Green onions, chopped
1/2	cup	Pimiento, chopped
1/3	cup	Vinegar
1/2	tsp	Dry mustard
1	clove	Garlic, crushed
		Salt and pepper
2/3	cup	Olive oil

-Combine together the peas, beans, celery, bell pepper, onions and pimiento.
-In a bowl combine the vinegar, mustard, garlic, salt and pepper.
-Gradually wisk in the olive oil.
-Pour over the vegetable mixture.
-Refrigerate and marinate several hours.
-Serve on a bed of lettuce.

SALADE TOMATE SAUCE CREOLE

TOMATO SALAD SAUCE CREOLE

A sharp spicy mustard is added to a basic vinaigrette dressing to marinate tomatoes, green onions and parsley for a refreshing and colorful salad.

1	bunch	Spinach or soft leaf lettuce
6		Tomatoes, sliced
6		Green onions, chopped
1/3	cup	Parsley, chopped
		Salt and pepper
1	tsp	Dijon mustard
1/3	cup	Vinegar
3/4	cup	Olive oil
1	tsp	Lemon juice

-Arrange spinach over a servng platter.
-Arrange tomatoes over spinach.
-Sprinkle with green onions and parsley.
-Blend together the salt, pepper, mustard, vinegar and lemon juice.
-Wisk in oil.

AVOCAT AU PAMPLEMOUSSE

AVOCADO AND GRAPEFRUIT SALAD

Tart grapefruit segments marinated in a vinaigrette sauce are the filling for avocado halves for a variation of filled avocados.

3		Avocados
3		Grapefruit
1/2	cup	Vinaigrette sauce
2	tsp	Parsley or mint, chopped

-Peel and remove the segments from the membrane of the grapefruit.
-Cut the avocado in half and remove the seed.
-Rub a little of the vinaigrette over the exposed flesh.
-Pour 1 tablespoon vinaigrette sauce in the center of each avocado.
-Blend gently the grapefruit with the remaining vinaigrette.
-Arrange the grapefruit segments over the avocado.
-Garnish with parsley or mint.
-Refrigerate 30 minutes.

SALADE DE PAMPLEMOUSSE ET DES CONCOMBRES

GRAPEFRUIT AND CUCUMBER SALAD

Another of those unusual and unexpected combinations which surprise the taste buds. Orange and lemon juice substitute for the vinegar in a classic vinaigrette to compliment the fruit and vegetable combination.

1/2	cup	Red onion, chopped
2	cups	Grapefruit sections
2	cups	Cucumbers, peeled, seeded and sliced
1		Lettuce, soft leaf
1		Orange, juiced
		Salt and pepper
1/2	tsp	Sugar
1/2	cup	Olive oil
1	tsp	Mint leaves, chopped (optional)

-Mix grapefruit, cucumbers and onions.
-Arrange on a bed of lettuce.
-In a bowl, blend the orange and lemon juices, salt, pepper and sugar.
-Gradually wisk in the olive oil.
-Add mint leaves if desired.
-Pour over the grapefruit and cucumbers.

SALADE PASTA PRIMAVERA

PASTA PRIMAVERA SALAD

In volume one we have a recipe for a main course dish called Pasta Primavera - pasta combined with green spring vegetables and a cream sauce - which is very popular in my classes. With a few changes in some of the ingredients, we have a cold salad which is great for a buffet for a large group.

1	cup	Broccoli
1	cup	Zucchini
1	cup	Green peas
1	cup	Mushrooms, sliced
1	cup	Cherry tomatoes, halved
1	cup	Pasta shells, small
2	tbs	Dijon mustard
2	tbs	Green onions, chopped
2	tbs	Parsley, chopped
1/3	cup	Wine vinegar
1	cup	cream
2	tbs	Lemon juice
		Salt and pepper

-Blanch broccoli, zucchini and green peas.
-Refresh in cold water.
-Boil pasta shells until al dente.
-Wash in cold water and drain.
-In a large bowl, blend together the mustard, onions, parsley, vinegar, cream, lemon juice, salt and pepper.
-Fold in the pasta shells.
-Fold in the vegetables.
-Place on a serving dish garnished with lettuce.

SALADE D'OLIVE ITALIENNE

ITALIAN OLIVE SALAD

My version of a famous New Orleans Italian salad used to make the well-known mufaletta sandwiches so popular in the French Quarter.

4	cups	Italian crushed olive salad mix
1 1/2	cups	Celery, chopped
1 1/2	cups	Dilled cauliflower
3/4	cup	Black olives, sliced
1 1/2	tbs	Oregano
1 1/2	cups	Olive oil
1	clove	Garlic
1/4	cup	Parsley, chopped
		Pepper

-Blend together the olive salad mix, cauliflower, and black olives.
-Wisk together the oregano, olive oil, garlic, parsley and pepper.
-Pour olive oil mixture over the vegetables.
-Mix well.
-Marinate several hours.

SALADE DES HUITRE

OYSTER SALAD

An unusual salad of cajun origin combines cabbage, eggs, celery, oysters and crackers soaked in the oyster liquid.

1	pt	Oysters
1	cup	Cabbage, shredded
		Mayonnaise
2		Hard cooked eggs
3		Sour pickles, chopped
1	cup	Cracker crumbs
1	cup	Celery

-Pour liquid from oysters over cracker crumbs.
-Parboil oysters, when cool chop fine.
-Add cracker crumbs, cabbage, celery and pickles.
-Season with mayonnaise.
-Serve over lettuce.
-Garnish with egg.

SALADE DE RIZ

RICE SALAD

An unusual combination which produces a great taste, cooked rice is blended with orange segments and green onions. Peanuts add a crunchy texture and mayonnaise binds it all together.

3	cups	Rice, cooked
1 1/2	cups	Manderine orange segments
4		Green onions
3/4	cup	Peanuts, unsalted
1 1/2	cup	Mayonnaise
		Salt and pepper

-Blend together the rice, orange segments and green onions.
-Add the peanuts, mayonnaise, salt and pepper.
-Blend all well.
-Chill.
-Serve on a bed of lettuce.

SAUCE VINAIGRETTE

VINAIGRETTE SAUCE

1/2	cup	Olive oil
1	clove	Garlic, crushed
3	tbs	Wine vinegar
1	tsp	Dijon mustard
1	tbs	Lemon juice
		Salt and pepper

-Blend together the garlic, vinegar, mustard, lemon juice, salt and pepper.
-Add the oil slowly while wisking vigorously.
-Makes about 3/4 cup.

SAUCE CREOLE

CREOLE DRESSING

The addition of a little brown Creole mustard and horseradish gives a classic vinaigrette that special taste called Creole.

2/3	cup	Olive oil
1/3	cup	Vinegar
1	tbs	Brown creole mustard
1	tbs	Horseradish
1/2	tsp	Sugar
		Salt and pepper

-Blend vinegar, mustard, horseradish, sugar, salt and pepper.
-Slowly beat in olive oil.
-Put some of the dressing over greens.
-Serve rest along side.

SAUCE A LA CREME FRANCAISE

CREAM FRENCH DRESSING

Cream is substituted for olive oil in the classic vinaigrette to create a creamy French dressing.

		Salt and pepper
1	tsp	Dijon mustard
2	tbs	Green onions, chopped
2	tsp	Parsley, chopped
6	tbs	Vinegar
2/3	cup	Cream
2	tsp	Lemon juice

-Combine salt, pepper, mustard, onions, parsley and vinegar in a bowl.
-Slowly wisk in the cream and the lemon juice.
-Blend thoroughly.

Soups

Gumbos

And

Chowders

SOUPS, GUMBOS AND CHOWDERS

SOUPE DES HUITRES ROCKERFELLER
    OYSTER SOUP ROCKERFELLER

BISQUE DES HUITRES
    OYSTER BISQUE

SOUPE DE CRABE
    CRAB SOUP

BISQUE DES CREVETTES
    SHRIMP BISQUE

VELOUTE NANTAIS
    CREAM OF SHRIMP SOUP NANTAIS

POTAGE DE POMME DE TERRE A LA ALLEMAGNE
    GERMAN POTATO SOUP

SOUP PORTUGAISE
    CABBAGE AND POTATO SOUP

VELOUTE D'OIGNON
    CREAM OF ONION SOUP

POTAGE DES ALLOBROGES
    ROOT VEGETABLE SOUP

SOUPE VERTE
    GREEN VEGETABLE SOUP

SOUPE DE BROCOLI AUX AMANDE
    BROCOLI SOUP ALMONDINE

GASPACHO SOUPE BLANCHE
    WHITE GASPACHO SOUP

SOUPS, GUMBOS AND CHOWDERS

Soups, gumbos, bisques and chowders are among my favorite foods. Ususally when I prepare one of the more hardy types I make large quantities so that I have some for the freezer. I also prepare them as main courses rather than as a first course. They are much too good for that. A good salad, some French bread and a light dessert and you have a splendid meal.

In Volume I we presented some of the classics -Creole Gumbo,. File Gumbo, Crawfish Bisque, Fish Chowder, Turkey Oyster Gumbo and my favorite Oyster Soup. In this volume we offer some more of this type of soup and begin with a variation of my favorite. I know you will enjoy it.

SOUPE DES HUITRES ROCKERFELLER

OYSTER SOUP ROCKERFELLER

This wonderful soup was first experienced at a restaurant in Opelousas, Louisiana. It is a variation of Oysters Rockerfeller and my Oyster Soup, both of which are in volume one.

1	qt	Oysters
2	tbs	Butter
2	tbs	Flour
2	cups	White onions, chopped
1 1/2	cups	Green onions, chopped
1/2	cup	Parsley, chopped
2	cups	Spinach, fresh, chopped
		OR
1	cup	Frozen spinach
4	oz	Butter
		Salt and pepper
1/2	oz	Pernod

-Drain oysters reserving liquid.
-Melt butter in a sauce pan.
-Add flour and cook two minutes.
-Add onions and cook until soft.
-Add green onions and parsley.
-Add water and reserved oyster liquid.
-Chop one half the oysters very fine.
-Add to soup mixture.
-Add spinach.
-Simmer for 30 minutes.
-Add remaining whole oysters, butter, salt and pepper.
-Simmer for another 15 minutes.
-Add Pernod.
-Cook for 1 minute longer.

BISQUE DES HUITRES

OYSTER BISQUE

Oysters simmered in light cream and seasoned with a Creole flare provides a soup worthy of being the main course.

3	tbs	Flour
4	tbs	Butter
4	cups	Oysters and their liquid
2	cups	Half and half cream
		Tabasco
		Salt and pepper
4	tbs	Sherry wine

-Make a light roux with the flour and butter.
-Add onions and saute for 2 or 3 minutes.
-Add the oyster liquid and the cream.
-Stir until thick.
-Add tabasco, salt and pepper.
-Chop half the oysters and add to the soup base.
-Add remaining whole oysters.
-Add sherry wine.
-Simmer for 10 to 12 minutes.

SOUPE DE CRABE

CRAB SOUP

The delicate taste of crab is enhanced yet preserved when served in this flavorful broth of seasoned cream. Rich and delicate.

1	lb	Lump crabmeat
1/4	cup	Dry sherry .
1		Green pepper, chopped
1	med	Onion, chopped
3	tbs	Butter
2	tbs	Flour
2	tsp	Chili powder
1/2	tsp	Sugar
2	cups	Cream

-In top of double boiler heat crab and sherry.
-In heavy skillet saute green pepper and onion in butter.
-Add flour, chili powder and sugar all blended.
-Cook slowly until it makes a roux.
-Add cream and stir until lightly thickened.
-Season with salt and pepper.
-Pour into double boiler with crab and sherry.
-Stir carefully.

BISQUE DES CREVETTES

SHRIMP BISQUE

A very old New Orleans recipe. Small balls of shrimp and aromatic vegetables are baked and served floating in the rich soup. You will love this one.

3	lbs	Shrimp, cleaned
1	cup	Onions, chopped
1/2	cup	Celery, chopped
2	tbs	Butter
2	tbs	Flour
1	qt	Water or shrimp stock
1	qt	Chicken stock
1	tbs	Tomato paste
1/2	cup	Bread crumbs
		Salt and pepper
1/2	cup	Green onions, chopped
1	tbs	Butter
1/3	cup	Bread crumbs
1		Egg yolk

-Grind shrimp in a food processor.
-Saute onions and celery in butter.
-Add flour and cook two minutes.
-Add water, stock, tomato paste and shrimp.
-Cook for 15 minutes.
-Add bread crumbs and blend well.
-Strain and return to low heat.
-Set half the shrimp mixture aside.
-Saute green onions in butter.
-Add shrimp mixture and bread crumbs.
-Remove from heat.
-Add egg yolk.
-Roll into small balls.
-Heat in oven for 5 minutes (350 degrees).
-Serve soup with two or three shrimp balls.

VELOUTE NANTAIS

CREAM OF SHRIMP SOUP NANTAIS

An unusual cream soup of shrimp, carrots, apples and wine. This delicious combination creates a wonderful taste sensation.

1	cup	Carrots, chopped
1	cup	Apples, chopped
2	oz	Butter
1 1/2	cups	Shrimp, shelled and deveined
1	tbs	Cognac
4	cups	White wine (Muscadet)
3	tbs	Flour
1	qt	Milk, heated
		Salt and pepper
2	oz	Shrimp, cooked (for garnish)

-Saute the carrots and apples in 1/2 the
    butter for 15 minutes.
-Add the shrimp.
-Baste with the cognac. (This should ignite.)
-Extinguish the flame with the white wine.
    Simmer 5 or 6 minutes.
-Make a light roux with the rest of the butter
    and the flour.
-Add the milk little by little.
-Salt and pepper.
-Add to the first preparation.
-Cook slowly for 25 minutes.

POTAGE DE POMME DE TERRE A LA ALLEMAGNE

GERMAN POTATO SOUP

Fresh tasting cucumbers and onions flavor a potato puree which is enriched with milk and cream then garnished with sausage.

2	lbs	Potatoes peeled and diced	-Boil potatoes in salted water until soft.
3	cups	Water	-Puree potatoes in a food mill with the boiling water.
1	tsp	Salt	-Return potatoes and water to pot and bring to a simmer.
2	sm	Cucumbers, peeled, seeded and diced	-Add cucumbers and onions.
1	sm	Onion, grated	-Blend in the milk and cream.
1	cup	Milk	-Add pepper to taste.
1	cup	Cream	-Simmer for 10 minutes.
		Pepper	-Add dill weed.
1	tsp	Dill weed	-Garnish with slices of Polish sausage if desired.
		Sliced Polish sausage, cooked (optional)	

SOUPE PORTUGAISE

CABBAGE AND POTATO SOUP

Potatoes and cabbage combine with garlic to produce a hardy soup with a Medeterranian flavor.

6	lg	Potatoes, peeled and sliced	-Cook potatoes and garlic in boiling, salt water for 15 minutes, covered, on a slow heat.
2	clove	Garlic, crushed	-Strain potatoes, reserving liquid.
6	qts	Water	-Put potatoes through a ricer.
1/2	head	Cabbage, sliced	-Return potatoes and reserved liquid to pot.
6	stems	Parsley, chopped	-Add cabbage.
1	tbs	Butter	-Continue cooking for 15 to 20 minutes.
		Salt and pepper	-At serving add butter and parsley.
			-Salt and pepper to taste.

VELOUTE D'OIGNON

CREAM OF ONION SOUP

The slow and long cooking of the onions develops their flavor, which is imparted to potatoes for a thick cream soup.

4	cups	Onions, sliced
4	tbs	Butter
1/2	cup	Flour
2	cups	Chicken stock
3	lg	Potatoes, boiled and mashed
4	cups	Milk, scalded
2	tbs	Parsley, chopped
1/4	cup	Celery leaves, chopped
		Salt
		White pepper

-Cook onions in butter slowly, covered for 15 minutes.
-Remove cover and cook another 15 or 20 minutes.
-Add flour and cook another 3 minutes.
-Add chicken stock and blend well.
-Add potatoes to scalded milk blending well.
-Add to the onion mixture.
-Add parsley, celery leaves, salt and pepper.
-Simmer for 10 to 12 minutes.

POTAGE DES ALLOBROGES

ROOT VEGETABLE SOUP

A combination of root vegetables - onions, leeks, turnips, celery root and potatoes - is the basis of this full body soup of country French origin.

2		Onions, chopped
2		Leeks, sliced thinly
2		Turnips, diced
1/2		Celery root, diced
2	lg	Potatoes, diced
		Salt and pepper
2	oz	Butter
1	qt	Water, boiling
1	pt	Milk, scaled
12	slice	French bread (Croutons)
5	oz	Swiss cheese

-Saute the onions in butter.
-Add the leeks, turnips and celery root.
-Cover and cook slowly for 15 minutes.
-Add the potatoes, salt and pepper.
-Add the water.
-Cover and cook 30 to 45 minutes more.
-Add the milk.
-Cook for 15 minutes.
-Saute the bread in butter.
-Cover each slice with cheese.
-To serve, place the croutons with cheese top of the soup.

To scald milk: Heat over low heat until tiny bubbles appear around the edge and surface films.

SOUPE VERTE

GREEN VEGETABLE SOUP

A combination of green vegetables - leeks, lettuce, green beans and green peas - is simmered slowly in chicken stock then enriched with cream to produce a flavorful dish.

1		Leek
10		Lettuce leaves, soft leaf type
1	cup	Green beans, sliced
1	cup	Green peas
2	oz	Butter
5	cups	Chicken stock
1	tbs	Flour
3	tbs	Cream
		Parsley, chopped
		Salt and pepper

-Cut the leek and lettuce leaves in julienne
   slices.
-Saute the leeks and lettuce in butter about
-Add the chicken stock and salt.
-Simmer 10 minutes.
-Drain, reserving liquid.
-Puree the vegetables.
-Return the puree and reserved liquid to the
   pot.
-Add the green peas and green beans.
-Cover and cook slowly for 20 minutes.
-Blend together the flour and cream.
-Mix with a little of the soup mixture.
-Add to the pot, mixing well.
-Continue cooking 5 minutes.
-Salt and pepper.
-At serving, garnish with parsley.

SOUPE DE BROCOLI AUX AMANDE

BROCCOLI SOUP ALMONDINE

This is a wonderful cold soup to be served during the hot months of summer and so it was on our special one hour holiday show for the Fourth of July. The soup is equally good served hot.

2	bunch	Broccoli
1/2	cup	Almonds
1 1/2	cups	Chicken stock, heated
4	tbs	Butter
2	tbs	Flour
2	tbs	Lemon juice
2	cups	Sour cream

-Cut flowerettes from broccoli.
-Peel stems and cut into pieces.
-Blanch in salted boiling water for 5 minutes
   (Reserve a few flowerettes).
-Place almonds, onions and broccoli into food
   processor or food mill.
-Process until smooth.
-Add 1/2 cup of chicken broth.
-Make a light roux with butter and flour.
-Add remaining chicken stock, lemon juice
   and sour cream.
-Add processed almonds and vegetables.
-Heat to boiling.
-At serving time garnish with reserved
   broccoli.
-Optional: Garnish with toasted almonds.

Variation: Do not refrigerate but serve hot. Toss reserved broccoli and almonds in butter until hot and garnish at serving time.

GASPACHO SOUPE BLANCHE

WHITE GASPACHO SOUP

We present here a soup of Spanish origin totally different from the tomato based Gaspacho soup in volume one. Almonds and garlic give this soup it's character.

1/2	cup	Blanched almonds
4	cloves	Garlic
1	tsp	Salt
1	cup	Bread, crust removed
1	cup	Olive oil
1/4	cup	White wine vinegar
1	tbs	Lemon juice
		Pepper
1	qt	Water

-Puree the almonds, garlic and salt.
-Soak bread in water then squeeze dry.
-Blend well with the almond mixture.
-Wisk in oil slowly until a mayonnaise is formed.
-Add vinegar, lemon juice and pepper.
-Wisk in the water.
-Chill.

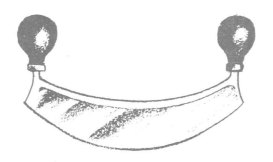

Aromatic vegetables are those which impart a flavor as well as an aroma to various food preparations. Some of the most often used are onions, garlic, carrots, celery, green onions and bell pepper. When cooked together and then blended with other ingredients they give the recipe character, flavor and fragrance. Onions, celery and bell pepper are called the holy trinity of Creole/Cajun cookery.

Use fresh garden herbs whenever possible. However dried herbs are excellent. Just remember that one tablespoon of chopped fresh herbs equals ½ teaspoon of dried.

A BEURRE MANIE is a blend of equal parts butter and flour used as a thickening agent. One tablespoon will thicken about 3/4 cup of liquid. Used mostly to correct the thickness of a roux based sauce.

Fish,

Crustaceans

And

Shellfish

FISH, CRUSTACEANS AND SHELLFISH

FILETS DES FLOUNDER PARISIENNE
SHRIMP STUFFED FLOUNDER FILLETS

CROQUETTES DE SAUMON
SALMON CROQUETTES

TRUITE AMANDINE
TROUT ALMONDINE

POISSON ROUGE CHAUD-FROID
RED SNAPPER CHAUD-FROID

FARCIS DES ECREVESSE
CRAWFISH STUFFING

CHAUD-FROID MAYONNAISE
MAYONNAISE COATING FOR FISH

CREVETTES A LA ROCKERFELLER
SHRIMP ROCKERFELLER

CREVETTES BOUILLI
BOILED SHRIMP

CREVETTES AMANDINE
SHRIMP ALMONDINE

CREVETTES ET CHAMPIGNONS-SAUCE ANETH
SHRIMP AND MUSHROOMS IN DILL SAUCE

CREVETTES ET·HUITRES CREOLE
SHRIMP AND OYSTER CREOLE

CREVETTES A LA TETRAZZINI
SHRIMP TETRAZZINI

CREVETTES FARCIES HOLLANDAISE
STUFFED SHRIMP HOLLANDAISE

FARCI DE CHAIR DE CRABE
CRAB MEAT STUFFING

CREVETTES A LA SAUCE BIERE
SHRIMP IN BEER SAUCE

CREVETTES GRILLEE
BARBECUED SHRIMP

CREVETTES FRITS A LA SAUCE BIERE
SHRIMP IN BEER BATTER

SAUCE PIQUANT
PUNGENT SAUCE

ETOUFEE DES ECREVESSE
CRAWFISH ETOUFEE

FUMET DE ECREVESSE
CRAWFISH STOCK

RAGOUT D'ECREVESSE
CRAWFISH STEW

SAUTE DE CRABE FINE BOUCHE
SAUTEED LUMP CRAB GOURMET

CRABE IMPERIAL
CRAB IMPERIAL

CHAIR DE CRABE CHANDELEUR
CRAB MEAT FEAST OF CANDLEMAS

COTES DES CRABES
CRAB CHOPS

CASSEROLE DE CHAIR DE CRABE
CRAB MEAT CASSEROLE

CRABE A LA ROMANOFF
CRAB MEAT WITH CAVIAR

CRABES MARINEE
MARINATED CRABS

CASSEROLE DES HUITRES
SCALLOPED OYSTERS

HUITRES AUX CARPES
OYSTERS IN CAPER SAUCE

HUITRES MONSIEUR LAFITTE
OYSTERS LAFITTE

MOULES MARINIERES
MUSSELS IN WHITE WINE

FISH, CRUSTACEANS AND SHELLFISH

We here on the Gulf Coast are very fortunate to have such an abundance of seafood available. However, since most freeze well and with today's rapid distribution system most people can enjoy these fruits of the sea with some regularity.

We present here some interesting dishes, especially the crawfish ones. This crustacean so popular with the Creoles and Cajuns of south Louisiana are now being shipped all over the US and the season has been extended by cultivation. I hope you will try and enjoy these dishes.

FILETS DES FLOUNDER PARISIENNE

SHRIMP STUFFED FLOUNDER FILLETS

Flounder fillets are stuffed with a shrimp mousse, rolled, poached and placed on a platter of sauce made with the poaching liquid.

8		Fillets of flounder or sole
		Juice of one lemon
		Salt and pepper
3/4	cup	Water
3/4	cup	White wine
2		Green onions, chopped
1/2	tsp	Tarragon
1	cup	Shrimp, shelled and deveined
		Salt and pepper
1	tsp	Dill weed
1/2	cup	Cream
1	cup	Small shrimp, shelled and deveined
1	tbs	Butter
1	cup	Cream

-Sprinkle fillet with lemon juice.
-Salt and pepper lightly.
-Set aside.
-Combine water, wine, green onions, salt and tarragon in a saucepan.
-Bring to a boil and simmer.
-Puree in a food processor the shrimp, any scraps of flounder available, salt, pepper and dill weed.
-Slowly add the cream.
-Spread some of the shrimp mousse on each fillet.
-Roll each fillet in jelly roll fashion.
-Wrap each fillet in plastic wrap.
-Place in a deep skillet.
-Strain water/wine liquid over fish.
-Cover with waxed paper.
-Poach 6 to 7 minutes.
-Remove and keep warm.
-Boil poaching liquid until reduced to 1/2 cup.
-In another saucepan cook shrimp in butter for 2 minutes.
-Add cream and bring to a boil.
-Add 1/2 cup poaching liquid.
-Return to a boil.
-Pour sauce onto a serving platter.
-Unwrap fish fillets and arrange over sauce.
-Garnish with sprigs of fresh dill or tarragon or chopped parsley.

POACHING LIQUID, often called AROMATIC BROTH or COURT BOUILLION is a liquid of either water, stock or wine, usually a combination of two or all of them and AROMATIC VEGETABLES and herbs used to poach or braise meats, fish or vegetables. Frequently, some of the liquid is used in the making of a sauce.

CROQUETTES DE SAUMON

SALMON CROQUETTES

These are especially good when served with lemon/caper sauce. Easy to make and they freeze well before frying.

1/2	cup	Onions, chopped	-Saute onions in butter until soft.
3	tbs	Butter	-Add flour and stir for 1 minute.
3	tbs	Flour	-Gradually add milk.
3/4	cup	Milk	-Cook until thick and smooth.
1		Egg, beaten	-Blend in the egg.
3	tbs	Parsley, chopped	-Add parsley, salt and cayenne.
		Salt	-Off heat fold in salmon.
1	pinch	Cayenne	-Add lemon juice.
3	cups	Canned salmon, bones and skin removed	-Lightly butter a jelly roll pan.
			-Cover with bread crumbs.
1	tsp	Lemon juice	-Spread salmon mixture over crumbs evenly.
		Bread crumbs	-Cover with more crumbs.
		Oil for frying	-Refrigerate until very cold.

-Pour oil into a skillet to about 1/4 inch deep.
-Heat over moderate to high heat.
-Cut salmon mixture into squares coating the edges with more bread crumbs.
-Fry in moderate to high heat until brown.
-Turn and brown the other side.
-Serve with lemon caper sauce.

TRUITE AMANDINE

TROUT ALMONDINE

Another classic, Trout Almondine is a simple but elegant method of preparing trout. Lemon, butter and almonds create an unforgetable sauce.

6	4oz	Speckled trout, fillets	-Soak fillets in milk 1 hour.
1	cup	Milk'	-Salt, pepper and flour fillets.
		Flour	-Saute fillets in margarine for about 6 minutes until golden.
1/2	lb	Margarine	
1/4	tsp	White pepper	-Transfer to oven proof dish and keep warm in a very slow oven.
1	tsp	Salt	
1/4	lb	Butter	-Melt butter in a skillet over moderate heat until slightly brown.
1/2	cup	Slivered almonds	-Add almonds and toss well.
1		Lemon	-Stir in lemon juice.
1	tbs	Parsley, chopped	-Arrange fillets on serving dish.

-Pour sauce over all.
-Decorate with lemon slices and chopped parsley.

POISSON ROUGE CHAUD-FROID

RED SNAPPER CHAUD-FROID

Our one hour Fourth of July show featured this beautiful red snapper stuffed with crawfish stuffing. After chilling, it was covered with a mayonnaise based cold sauce and garnished with vegetable flowers. Not only a sight to behold but delicious.

1	6-lb	Red snapper
1	recipe	Crawfish stuffing
1	recipe	Chaud-froid mayonnaise

-Have fishmonger scale, clean and remove
the eyes and gills from snapper.
-Wash thoroughly.
-Lay snapper on a jelly roll pan diagonally
with tail extending over the edge.
-Fill cavity with stuffing and enclose with a
double thickness of aluminum foil.
-Cover tail and fins with foil.
-Place a ball of foil in fish's mouth.
-Sprinkle with lemon juice.
-Brush lightly with peanut oil.
-Bake in a 375 degree oven for 45 minutes
(approx. 8 min. per lb.).
-Remove from oven and allow to cool.
-Place in refrigerator, covered loosoly for 3 or
more hours.
-Remove fromoosely for 3 or more hours.
-Remove from refrigerator.
-Remove foil.
-Remove skin from body of fish.
-With a spatula and a pastry brush cover the
body of the fish with chaud-froid mayonnaise.
-Garnish the fish with vegetable flower cut
outs.
-Refrigerate until ready to serve.
-Place jelly roll pan with fish on a large serving
tray.
-Surround fish with parsley sprigs.
-Garnish the tray with one of the following:
   1. Whole boiled crayfish.
   2. Whole boiled shrimp.
   3. Boiled peeled shrimp.
   4. Small boiled crabs.
   5. Stuffed mushrooms.
   6. Blanched cold asparagus.
   7. Marinated artichoke hearts.
   8. Radish roses.

FARCIS DES ECREVESSE

CRAWFISH STUFFING

1	cup	Onions, chopped
1	lb	Crawfish tails
2	slices	French bread
1	lg	Egg, beaten
		Salt and pepper
1/2	cup	Parsley, chopped
2	cloves	Garlic, chopped

-Saute onions in a small amount of oil until well done.
-Chop crawfish tails.
-Add to onions.
-Soak bread in 1/2 cup water and squeeze dry.
-Add to onions/crawfish.
-Blend in egg.
-Add salt, pepper, parsley and garlic.
-Blend all well.
-Cook until mixture holds a shape.

Variations: Substitute one of the following for the crawfish: 1. Boiled crab meat (1 lb.) 2. Boiled shrimp (1 lb. tail meat.) 3. Cooked fish, flaked (2 cups) 4. Fresh oysters, chopped (2 cups plus 1 cup crushed crackers). 5. Combination of your choice of the above. (1 lb. or 2 cups).

CHAUD-FROID MAYONNAISE

MAYONNAISE COATING FOR FISH

1	tbs	Unflavored gelatin
1/4	cup	Cold water
2	tbs	Heavy cream
3	cups	Mayonnaise at room temperature

-Soak gelatin in cold water.
-Warm over low heat to dissolve.
-Add cream.
-Stir in the mayonnaise.
-Allow to cool slightly.
-Brush on very cold food to glaze.

CRUSTACEANS

CREVETTES A LA ROCKERFELLER

SHRIMP ROCKERFELLER

A variation of the classic oysters Rockerfeller created by Antoine's in New Orleans. Boiled shrimp are enrobed with a sauce of spinach and aromatic vegetables and baked.

1	cup	Green onions, chopped finely
2	cloves	Garlic, chopped
4	oz	Butter
1/2	cup	Celery, chopped
1/2	cup	Parsley, chopped
3	cups	Spinach, blanched and chopped
1	cup	Lettuce, blanched and chopped
		Salt and pepper
3	drops	Tabasco
1	tbs	Worchestershire sauce
3	slices	Bread
1/2	cup	White wine
1	oz	Pernod (optional)
1	recipe	Boiled shrimp (2 lbs)
6		Scallop shells
2	tbs	Butter, melted
3/4	cup	Bread crumbs
1/4	cup	Parmesan cheese

-Saute onions and garlic in butter.
-Add celery, parsley, spinach and lettuce.
-Mix well in the butter.
-Add salt, pepper, tabasco and worchestershire sauce.
-Soak bread in the wine.
-Add to the vegetables.
-Cook until thickened.
-Add the Pernod.
-Lightly butter the scallop shells.
-Reserve 12 to 18 shrimp for each shell.
-Half fill the shells with the remaining shrimp.
-Cover with the vegetable mixture.
-Combine butter and bread crumbs.
-Sprinkle each shell with bread crumbs and cheese.
-Place 2 or 3 reserved shrimp on top of each shell.
-Bake in a 400 degree oven for 10 to 12 minutes.

CREVETTES BOUILLI

BOILED SHRIMP

4	qts	Water
1		Onion, sliced
1		Lemon, sliced
		Salt and pepper
3	tbs	Crab boil liquid
2	lbs	Shrimp, headless

-Place onion, lemon, salt and pepper in the water.
-Bring to a boil.
-Add shrimp.
-Return to a simmer.
-Simmer 5 to 7 minutes based on the size of the shrimp.
-Remove from heat.
-Pour two cups cold water over.
-Let rest 15 minutes.
-Drain.
-Peel and devein.

CREVETTES AMANDINE

SHRIMP ALMONDINE

Shrimp are marinated in an aromatic marinade of oil, lemon and garlic which becomes the basis of a sauce garnished with almonds.

3	lbs	Shrimp, cleaned & deveined
1/2	cup	Olive oil
3	tbs	Peanut oil
1/2	cup	Lemon juice
6	tbs	Butter
2	cloves	Garlic, chopped
1	cup	Slivered almonds
2	dashes	Tabasco
4	tbs	Vermouth
1/2	cup	Green onions, chopped
		Salt and pepper

-Marinate shrimp in olive oil, peanut oil, lemon juice and garlic about 2 hours.
-Reserve sauce.
-Melt butter in a skillet.
-Saute shrimp and green onions about 6 minutes.
-Remove shrimp and onions and place on a warm serving platter.
-Add almonds, salt and reserved marinade to the skillet.
-Add tabasco and wine.
-Simmer for 3 or 4 minutes.
-Pour over the shrimp.

> **It takes 1 1/2 pounds of shrimp with heads on to yield one pound of cleaned and shelled tails.**

CREVETTES ET CHAMPIGNONS - SAUCE ANETH

SHRIMP AND MUSHROOMS IN DILL SAUCE

A very old recipe given to me by a very dear friend from New Orleans. It never fails to get raves and requests for copies of the recipe.

2	lbs	Shrimp, raw and cleaned
1/2	lb	Mushrooms, sliced
2	tbs	Butter
		Salt and pepper
1/4	cup	Brandy
1 1/2	cups	Heavy cream
2		Egg yolks, beaten
		Cayenne pepper
		Juice of 1 lemon
3	tbs	Dill weed

-Heat butter in a saucepan.
-Add mushrooms.
-Cook about 2 minutes.
-Add shrimp.
-Salt and pepper to taste.
-Cook about 3 to 4 minutes.
-Pour brandy over.
-Ignite.
-Remove shrimp and mushrooms.
-Add cream to skillet.
-Cook over high heat 6 minutes.
-Blend in egg yolks.
-Return shrimp and mushrooms to sauce.
-Cook briefly.
-Add cayenne to taste, lemon juice and dill weed.
-Serve with boiled rice.

CREVETTES ET HUITRES CREOLE

SHRIMP AND OYSTER CREOLE

Shrimp and oysters combine to create a variation of a New Orleans Shrimp Creole. The use of a stock made from the shrimp shells and the oyster liquid provides a unique flavor.

1	lg	Onion, sliced
3	lbs	Shrimp, shelled and deveined
		Shrimp heads and shells from above
1	pt	Oysters, drained
		Oyster liquid from above oysters
3	tbs	Butter
1	tbs	Peanut oil
1	tbs	Flour
2	cups	Onions, chopped
1	cup	Celery, diced
1	cup	Green pepper, diced
1	clove	Garlic, minced
1	tbs	Vinegar
		Salt and cayenne.
3		Bay leaves
1	tsp	Thyme
1	can	Tomatoes (16 oz)
2	cups	Frozen green peas
3	tbs	Parsley, chopped

-Cover onions and shrimp heads with water and oyster liquid.
-Simmer 30 minutes.
-Strain and set aside.
-Saute onions in butter and oil until well done.
-Add flour and cook about 2 minutes.
-Add onions, celery, green pepper and garlic.
-Saute until soft.
-Add vinegar, salt, cayenne, bay leaves and thyme.
-Add tomatoes and their juices.
-Add one cup of stock reserved above.
-Bring to a boil.
-Simmer for 15 to 20 minutes.
-Add shrimp, oysters and green peas.
-Simmer 5 minutes more.
-Garnish with parsley.
-Serve with boiled rice.

CREVETTES A LA TETRAZZINI

SHRIMP TETRAZZINI

Chicken Tetrazzini is a well-known and popular dish, a recipe for which can be found in the poultry chapter. This version using shrimp instead of chicken is delicious and a welcome variation.

1/2	cup	Flour
4	tbs	Butter
3	cups	Milk
		Salt and pepper
1/2	lb	Cheddar cheese
1/2	lb	Mushrooms
1/2	cup	Sherry
1	lb	Spaghetti, cooked al dente
3	lbs	Shrimp, boiled and shelled
1/2	cup	Bread crumbs
3	tbs	Butter, melted

-Cook flour in butter for 2 minutes.
-Add milk and blend well.
-Salt and pepper.
-Add cheese and blend until melted and sauce is thick.
-Saute mushrooms in a little butter.
-Add sherry wine.
-In a baking dish (2 1/2 qt.) make a layer with the pasta.
-Cover with the shrimp.
-Place mushrooms over shrimp.
-Pour sauce over all.
-Sprinkle with bread crumbs.
-Drizzle the butter over crumbs.
-Bake at 350 degrees for 30 minutes.

CREVETTES FARCIES HOLLANDAISE

STUFFED SHRIMP HOLLANDAISE

Another New Orleans favorite, large butterfly shrimp are filled with a seasoned crab stuffing coated with bread crumbs and deep fried. Serve with a hollandaise sauce.

1 1/2	lbs	Shrimp, large and headless	
2		Eggs	
1	cup	Milk	
1	cup	Flour	
2	cups	Bread crumbs, seasoned	
1	recipe	Crab dressing	
1	recipe	Hollandaise	

-Peel shrimp, leaving tails on.
-Split down back, remove vein, and butterfly.
-Place a small amount of dressing in each shrimp.
-Press firmly to shape.
-Blend eggs and flour together.
-Roll shrimp in flour.
-Place in egg wash.
-Roll in bread crumbs.
-Fry in deep, hot (325-350) peanut oil until golden, about 2 minutes.
-Serve with Hollandaise sauce on side.

When frying chicken, oysters, shrimp or fish, add several drops of Tabasco sauce to the oil. Add while cold to prevent splattering.

FARCI DE CHAIR DE CRABE

CRAB MEAT STUFFING

6		Green onions, chopped
3/4	cup	White onion, chopped
4	cloves	Garlic, chopped
1/4	lb	Butter
2		Bay leaves
3	tbs	Flour
1	cup	Milk, heated
		Salt and pepper
1/2	lb	Crab meat
1/2	cup	Bread crumbs
1		Egg, beaten

-Saute in the butter, the green onions, white onions, garlic and bay leaves.
-Remove bay leaves.
-Add flour blending well.
-Add milk and stir until sauce thickens.
-Add salt and pepper.
-Fold in crab meat.
-Add bread crumbs and mix well.
-Add egg and blend.
-Cool.

CREVETTES ETOUFEE

This Creole dish is a variation of crawfish etoufee. It combines shrimp with green onions, celery, bell pepper and garlic along with herbs and spices to create a memorable meal.

2	cups	Shrimp stock	-Heat stock and set aside.
3	tbs	Peanut oil	-Make a very dark roux by cooking the flour in the oil and butter about 20 minutes.
3	tbs	Butter	
1/2	cup	Flour	-Add onions, green onions, celery, bell pepper, garlic, thyme, basil, tomato paste, pepper, salt and worchestershire.
1/2	cup	Onions, chopped	
1/2	cup	Green onions, chopped	
1/2	cup	Celery, chopped	-Cook vegetables and seasonings for about 5 minutes.
1/4	cup	Bell pepper	
1	tsp	Garlic, chopped	-Add heated stock and blend well.
1/4	tsp	Thyme	-Cook until thick like cream.
1/2	tsp	Basil	-Add shrimp tail meat.
2	tbs	Tomato paste	-Heat thoroughly.
1/2	tsp	Cayenne pepper	-Remove from heat.
1	tsp	Salt	-Add parsley and green onions.
1	tbs	Worchestershire	-Serve over boiled rice.
2	lbs	Shrimp tail meat, cooked and deveined	
2	tbs	Parsley, chopped	
1/2	cup	Green onions, chopped	

CREVETTES GRILLEE

Although called barbecued, these shrimp are actually baked with butter and seasonings. They are best baked in the shells and peeled by each individual when eaten. You will need crusty French bread to soak up the sauce.

2-3	lbs	Shrimp	-Lay shrimp flat in baking pan.
1/2	lb	Butter	-Cover generously with black pepper, salt and garlic powder.
		Garlic powder	
		Salt and pepper	-Add butter.
		Paprika	-Sprinkle with paprika.
			-Bake in 350 degree oven for 35 minutes turning frequently.

NOTE: Shrimp can be cleaned and deveined or can be baked in shells.

CREVETTES FRITS A LA SAUCE BIERE

SHRIMP IN BEER BATTER

Beer provides a unique flavor to the batter for these deep fried butterflied shrimp. The sauce is great.

24		Jumbo shrimp	
1	12oz	Bottle beer	
1	tsp	Salt	
1 1/2	cups	Flour	

-Butterfly shrimp.
-Combine beer, salt and flour, blending until smooth. Batter should be thick but not pasty.
-Dust shrimp with flour.
-Dip in beer batter.
-Deep fry at 350 degrees for about 5 minutes until golden brown.
-Serve with pungent sauce.

SAUCE PIQUANT

PUNGENT SAUCE

1	cup	Orange marmalade
1	tsp	Ginger
1	oz	Lemon juice
2	tbs	Horseradish sauce

-Blend all ingredients in a blender.

One pound of head on shrimp will yield 15 to 20 jumbo, 20 to 25 large, 25-30 medium and 35-45 small.

CREVETTES A LA SAUCE BIERE

SHRIMP IN BEER SAUCE

A unique recipe for shrimp cooked in a sauce made from beer and tapioca.

3	lbs	Shrimp, shelled and deviened
1		Red onion, chopped
1	clove	Garlic
3	tbs	Olive oil
1	tsp	Salt
2	cups	Beer
1/3	cup	Lemon juice
1/2	tsp	Oregano
2	tbs	Minute tapioca
1/4	cup	Chopped parsley
		Cayenne pepper

-Add chopped onion and garlic to hot olive oil and saute until transparent.
-Add shrimp, salt, cayenne, beer, lemon juice and oregano.
-Stirring constantly, bring to a boil and simmer until shrimp are firm and pink (about 5-7 minutes).
-Drain liquid off shrimp and reserve.
-Pour over tapioca stirring constantly.
-Simmer to consistency of good sauce.
-Return shrimp to sauce.
-Garnish with parsley.

ETOUFEE DES ECREVESSE

CRAWFISH ETOUFEE

Over the years I have avoided using ingredients on the show not readily available and crawfish was one of them. However, thanks to the majic cajun Chef Paul Proudhomme the Louisiana crawfish have become popular and more readily available. Here is a classic of the Cajun repetoire.

2	cups	Crawfish stock
3	tbs	Peanut oil
3	tbs	Butter
1/2	cup	Flour
1/2	cup	Onions, chopped
1/2	cup	Green onions, chopped
1/2	cup	Celery, chopped
1/4	cup	Bell pepper
1	tsp	Garlic, chopped
1/4	tsp	Thyme
1/2	tsp	Basil
2	tbs	Tomato paste
1/2	tsp	Cayenne pepper
1	tsp	Salt
1	tbs	Worchestershire
2	lbs	Crawfish tails plus their fat
2	tbs	Parsley, chopped
1/2	cup	Green onions, chopped

-Heat stock and set aside.
-Make a very dark roux by cooking the flour in the oil and butter about 20 minutes.
-Add onions, green onions, celery, bell pepper, garlic, thyme, basil, tomato paste, pepper, salt and Worchestershire.
-Cook vegetables and seasonings for about 5 minutes.
-Add heated stock and blend well.
-Cook until thick like cream.
-Add crawfish tails and their fat.
-Heat thoroughly.
-Remove from heat.
-Add parsley and green onions.
-Serve over boiled rice.

FUMET DE ECREVESSE

CRAWFISH STOCK

		Heads and shells of crawfish
1		Onion, chopped
1/2	cup	Celery tops
4	cups	Water

-Combine crawfish heads and shells with onion, celery tops and water in a stock pot.
-Bring to a boil then simmer about 20 to 30 minutes.
-Strain.

RAGOUT D'ECREVENISSE

CRAWFISH STEW

A creole dish with exceptional flavor. It can also be made with uncooked shrimp using shrimp stock.

2	cups	Onions, chopped
2	cups	Celery, chopped
1	cup	Bell pepper, chopped
2	cloves	Garlic
6	oz	Tomato paste
3	cups	Crawfish tail meat
		Salt and pepper
1 1/2	cup	Crawfish stock or water
1/4	cup	Green onion tops, chopped
1/2	cup	Parsley, chopped

-Saute onions and celery in oil until onions turn brown over medium heat.
-Add bell pepper and garlic.
-Add tomato paste.
-Cook about 3 to 4 minutes stirring constantly.
-Add crawfish, salt and pepper.
-Add stock or water to obtain a thickness that coats the back of a spoon.
-Simmer about 15 minutes.
-Add green onion tops and parsley.
-Cook 5 minutes longer.
-Serve over rice.

It takes eight pounds of boiled crawfish to produce one pound of tail meat.

SAUTE DE CRABE FINE BOUCHE

SAUTEED LUMP CRAB GOURMET

Crab meat is combined with mushrooms, bell peppers and seasonings to produce a dish that can truly be called gourmet.

1	cup	Mushrooms, sliced
1/2	cup	Green pepper, chopped
2	oz	Pimientos
8	tbs	Butter
2	lbs	Lump crab meat
		Salt
		Cayenne
1/2	tsp	Leaf thyme
2	cups	Heavy cream
1/3	cup	Brandy, heated

-Saute mushrooms, peppers and pimientos in 3 tbs butter until tender.
-In another saucepan, saute crab meat in the rest of the butter.
-Sprinkle with salt and pepper.
-Pour the brandy over it and ignite.
-Add thyme and cook over low heat for 10 minutes.
-Stir in mushrooms and peppers.
-Serve from a chafing dish or in individual ramekins.

To slice mushrooms quickly and in even slices use an egg slicer.

CRABE IMPERIAL

CRAB IMPERIAL

Spicy homemade mayonnaise holds the crab meat baked in shells for an imperial taste.

4		Egg yolks (at room temperature)
1/4	cup	Lemon juice
2	tsp	Dry mustard
3	tsp	Worchestershire
		Generous dash of tabasco
		Salt and white pepper to taste
3	cups	Olive oil
2	lbs	Crab meat
		Melted butter
		Paprika

-Combine first 6 ingredients in a bowl.
-Add oil, beating constantly, until mixture is thick and smooth.
-Add crab meat and mix.
-Heap in shells and brush with melted butter.
-Sprinkle with paprika and bake in a 350 degree oven 15-20 minutes.
-Serve hot.

CHAIR DE CRABE CHANDELEUR

CRAB MEAT FEAST OF CANDLEMAS

Aromatic vegetables, tomatoes and clam juice are reduced to concentrate flavors and added to mayonnaise for an unusual sauce to accompany crab meat.

3/4	cup	Onion, chopped
4	tbs	Butter
2	cloves	Garlic, minced
2	lb	Tomatoes, peeled, seeded and chopped
1		Bay leaf
1/2	tsp	Tarragon
1 1/2	cup	Clam broth
1 1/2	cup	Mayonnaise
		Salt and pepper
2	lb	Lump crab meat

-Saute onions in butter until soft.
-Add garlic, tomatoes, bay leaf and clam broth.
-Simmer until reduced to 1 cup.
-Remove from heat.
-Cool.
-Remove bay leaf.
-Blend in mayonnaise.
-Add salt and pepper to taste.
-Gently stir in crab meat.
-Cook over low heat until crab is heated. Do not boil.
-Serve over rice.

COTES DES CRABES

CRAB CHOPS

Your eyes may be fooled by crab meat stuffing made to look like a pork chop but your taste buds will be excited. Serve this with the Lemon Caper Sauce from the sauce chapter.

4	tbs	Butter
1/3	cup	Flour
6		Green onions, chopped
1/3	cup	Parsley, chopped
3/4	cup	Milk
2		Eggs, beaten
1/8	tsp	Cayenne pepper
1/8	tsp	Mace
		Salt and pepper
1	tsp	Worchestershire sauce
1	lb	Crab meat
		Bread crumbs
2		Eggs
1	tbs	Water
		Cracker meal

-Melt butter in a skillet.
-Add flour and make a light roux.
-Add green onions and parsley.
-Cook about 2 to 3 minutes.
-Add beaten eggs blending well.
-Add cayenne, mace, salt, pepper and worchestershire sauce.
-Blend in crab meat and enough bread crumbs
  to thicken, about 4 tablespoons.
-Cool until able to handle.
-Shape to resemble pork chops dipping hands in bread crumbs.
-Coat well with bread crumbs.
-Chill for 3 to 4 hours.
-Dip each chop in beaten egg mixed with the water.
-Coat well with cracker meal.
-Fry in a small amount of butter and oil until golden on both sides.
-Garnish with lemon.

CASSEROLE DE CHAIR DE CRABE

CRAB MEAT CASSEROLE

Artichoke hearts, crab and swiss cheese are layered with a white sauce to create a tasty casserole for gourmet tastes.

5	tbs	Flour
5	tbs	Butter
1	cup	Green onions, chopped
1 1/2	cups	Milk, heated
4-5	drops	Tabasco sauce
		Salt and pepper
2	cans	Artichoke hearts, halved
2	lbs	Crab meat
1	cup	Swiss cheese, grated
		Bread crumbs, seasoned

-Cook flour in butter for 2 minutes.
-Add green onions and cook for 1 minute.
-Blend in milk to form a bechamel sauce.
-Add tabasco.
-Season with salt and pepper.
-Cool.
-Layer artichoke hearts, crab meat and cheese in a baking dish.
-Pour bechamel sauce over the layers.
-Sprinkle with bread crumbs.
-Bake at 350 degrees for 30 minutes.

CRABE A LA ROMANOFF

CRAB MEAT WITH CAVIAR

An elegant first course or luncheon entree is this delicate but rich combination of crab, hollandaise and caviar.

1	lb	Lump crab meat
1/4	cup	Brandy
1/4	cup	Dry sherry
1	cup	Cream
1	cup	Sauce hollandaise
		Salt to taste
1/2	tsp	Cayenne pepper
3	oz	Caviar
4		Slices buttered toast

-In a skillet or chafing dish add crab and brandy.
-Ignite brandy.
-Add sherry and cream.
-Stir gently.
-Add hollandaise.
-Blend well.
-Add salt and pepper.
-Add caviar.
-Mix well but gently.
-Serve over toast.

CRABES MARINEE

What fun it is to pick and eat these boiled crabs marinated in oil, vinegar and seasonings on a summer evening with iced cold beer.

1	doz	Boiled crabs
1	cup	Olive oil
1/3	cup	Wine vinegar
4	cloves	Garlic, minced
1	tsp	Dry mustard
1	tsp	Horseradish
1	tbs	Worcestershire
		Juice of 2 lemons
1	rib	Celery, chopped
1	sm	Green pepper, chopped
1	med	Onion, chopped
3		Green onions, chopped
2	tbs	Parsley, chopped
		Salt and pepper

-Remove crab claws and crack them.
-Clean bodies, break in half, retain feelers.
-Blend oil, vinegar, garlic, mustard, horseradish, worcestershire and lemon juice.
-Add celery, green pepper, onion, green onions, and parsley.
-Salt and pepper to taste.
-Pour over crabs in an enamal or stainless container.
-Marinate in refrigerator at least 24 hours.
-Stir occasionally.
-Will keep about a week.

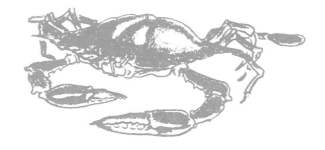

SHELLFISH

CASSEROLE DES HUITRES

SCALLOPED OYSTERS

Aromatic vegetables are combined with crackers, milk and oyster liquid in a casserole and sprinkled with cheese to create a baked casserole any oyster lover will enjoy.

1	qt	Oysters
1	cup	Green onions, chopped
1/2	cup	Celery, chopped
4	tbs	Butter
3	tbs	Parsley, chopped
2	cloves	Garlic, chopped
2	tsp	Lemon juice
		Salt and pepper
3/4	cup	Milk
2 1/2	cups	Sweet crackers, crushed
1/2	cup	Cheddar cheese, grated

-Simmer oysters in their liquid until edges curl.
-Drain reserving liquid.
-Saute onions and celery in butter until tender.
-Add parsley, garlic, lemon juice, salt and pepper.
-Add 1/2 cup reserved oyster liquid and the milk.
-Add oysters.
-Blend in 2 cups of the sweet cracker crumbs.
-Pour into a 1 1/2 quart casserole.
-Mix together the cheese and the remaining cracker crumbs.
-Sprinkle over casserole.
-Bake at 375 degrees for 15 to 20 minutes.

HUITRES AUX CARPES

OYSTERS IN CAPER SAUCE

An excellent first course or a luncheon entree when served in scallop shells.

3	doz	Oysters
3 1/2	tbs	Butter
1 1/4	cups	Celery, chopped
3 1/2	tbs	Flour
1/4	cup	Capers, drained and chopped
3 1/2	tbs	Cream
3 1/2	tbs	Butter, melted
1/3	cup	Fine bread crumbs

-Heat oysters in liquid. Do not boil.
-Drain and measure 1 3/4 cups liquid.
-Melt butter in saucepan - medium heat.
-Saute celery until tender but crisp.
-Add flour and stir until blended.
-Add oyster liquid gradually and cook, stirring constantly until sauce thickens.
-Remove from heat.
-Add capers and cream.
-Add oysters.
-Spoon into shells or ramikins.
-Mix the butter with crumbs.
-Sprinkle over oysters.
-Bake in 450 degree for 10 minutes.

HUITRES MONSIEUR LAFITTE

OYSTERS LAFITTE

Mushrooms and shrimp in an aromatic sauce are placed over oysters on the half shell for a flavorful baked oyster dish.

1/4	cup	Butter
1/4	cup	Chopped shallots or green onions
2	cups	Chopped mushrooms
1/4	cup	Chopped parsley
1	cup	Chopped, cooked shrimp
1	clove	Garlic, minced
1/2	cup	Dry white wine
2	dozen	Oysters on the half shell, drained, liquid reserved
1/2	tsp	Salt
	dash	Cayenne
1	cup	Heavy cream
1	tbs	Melted butter
2	tbs	Flour
		Rock salt
2	tbs	Bread crumbs
2	tbs	Butter

-Heat 1/4 cup butter in skillet over medium heat.
-Add shallots or green onions, mushrooms, parsley, shrimp and garlic.
-Cook 1 minute.
-Add wine, oyster liquid, salt and cayenne.
-Bring to boiling.
-Simmer 1 minute.
-Stir in cream.
-Blend 1 tablespoon melted butter with flour until smooth.
-Add to mushroom-shrimp mixture, stirring until sauce has thickened.
-Correct seasoning to taste.
-Heat oven to 450 degrees.
-Arrange oysters on a bed of rock salt in an ovenproof platter.
-Place about 2 tablespoons of shrimp mixture over each oyster.
-Sprinkle with bread crumbs.
-Dot with butter.
-Bake 15 to 20 minutes.

MOULES MARINIERES

MUSSELS IN WHITE WINE

So simple and so delicious, this classically French dish cooks mussels in wine, onion, garlic and seasonings. The mussel juices combine with the wine to form a delicious sauce. Lots of French bread will be needed.

2	qts	Mussels
1	pt	Dry white wine
4		Green onions
1	clove	Garlic
2		Bay leaves
1	tsp	Thyme, leaf type
2	tbs	Parsley, chopped
4	tbs	Butter
		Salt and pepper, to taste

-Clean mussel shells scrubbing well.
-Melt butter in a saucepan.
-Add onions and garlic.
-Cook for 2 minutes.
-Add wine and bring to a boil.
-Add salt and pepper.
-Add mussels, thyme and parsley.
-Turn mussels constantly for 3 or 4 minutes until all the mussels open.
-Remove the mussels.
-Reduce the cooking liquid by half.
-Return the mussels to liquid.
-Serve in soup bowls with French bread to sop up the juice.

Beef, Veal,
Pork and Lamb

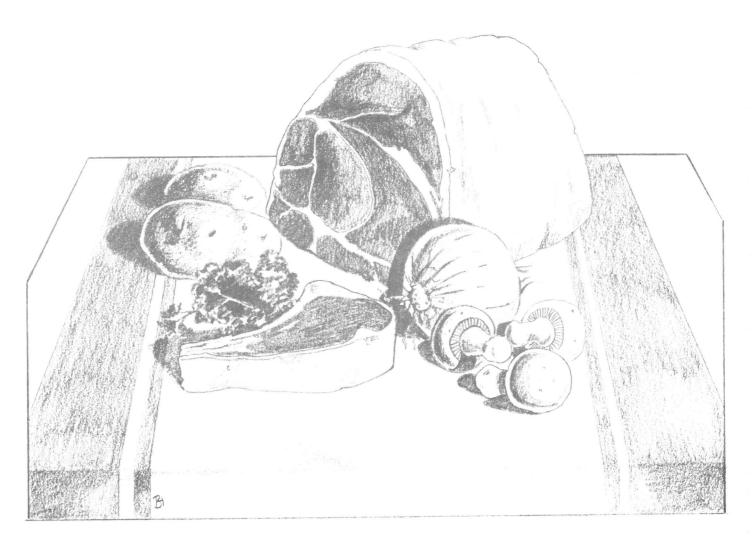

BEEF, VEAL, PORK AND LAMB

BOEUF FARCI A LA SAUCE HUITRES
STUFFED FLANK WITH OYSTER SAUCE

SAUCE D'HUITRES
OYSTER SAUCE

BOEUF AUX OLIVES
BEEF AND OLIVES IN RED WINE SAUCE

BOULETTES DE VIANDE A L'ITALIENNE
VEAL MEAT BALLS ITALIAN STYLE

BOEUF AU POIVRON ET AUX CHAMPIGNONS
BRAISED BEEF, PEPPERS AND MUSHROOMS

RAGOUT DE BOEUF A LA GRECQUE
BEEF STEW GREEK STYLE

HACHIS PARMENTIER
BEEF AND POTATOES AU GRATIN

CROQUETTE DE BOEUF EN SAUCE TOMATE
BEEF CROQUETTES IN TOMATO SAUCE

HAMBURGERS A LA CREME D'OIGNONS
HAMBURGERS WITH CREAMED ONIONS

COTE DE PORC AUX CERISES
PORK CHOPS WITH CHERRIES

DAUBE DE PORC AUX POIVRONS
BRAISED PORK AND PEPPERS WITH NOODLES

COTE DE PORC SAUCE DIABLE
SAUTEED PORK FILETS-DEVIL SAUCE

COTE DE PORC AUX POMMES
PORK CHOPS WITH APPLES

ROTI DE PORC EN COURONNE
CROWN ROAST OF PORK

FARCIS DES CANNEBERGES, NOIX ET RIZ
CRANBERRY, PECAN, RICE STUFFING

ESCALOPES DE PORC GRATINEES
PORK AND MUSHROOMS GRATIN

CHOU FARCI A LA NICOISE
STUFFED CABBAGE NICOISE

SAUCE TOMATE
TOMATO SAUCE

TRANCHES DE JAMBON ROULE AUX PECHES
HAM ROLLS WITH PEACHES

BEIGNETS DE JAMBON
HAM AND CHEESE FRITTERS

TRANCHES DE JAMBON FINES BOUCHES
HAM STEAKS GOURMET

GIDOT D'AGNEAU FARCI AUX ABRICOTS
LEG OF LAMB STUFFED WITH APRICOTS

BEEF, VEAL, PORK AND LAMB

In Volume I we presented a variety of meat dishes that tended to be from the classic group. Here in volume II we demonstrate recipes of a more humble origin. Sometimes the humble or country cooking proves to be the best and most tasty. We present several interesting dishes for ground meats such as Beef Croquettes and for meats with fruit - Pork with Cherries. I hope they will please you.

BOEUF FARCI A LA SAUCE HUITRES

STUFFED FLANK WITH OYSTER SAUCE

A spicy stuffing, ham, oysters, aromatic vegetables and bread, in the creole style, is rolled jelly roll fashion in a beef flank and is braised in beef stock. An oyster sauce accompanies each slice when served.

2	tbs	Butter	-Saute onions in butter until soft.
1	cup	Onions, chopped	-Add ham, bread crumbs and oysters.
1	cup	Ham, chopped	-Add garlic, parsley, thyme, sage and
1	cup	Bread crumbs	pepper.
1/2	cup	Oysters, chopped	-Blend in egg.
1	clove	Garlic	-Set aside.
1/4	cup	Parsley, chopped	-Butterfly steak by cutting horizontally to
1/2	tsp	Thyme	within 1/2 inch of other side.
1/2	tsp	Sage	-Open steak like a book.
		Salt and pepper	-Spread stuffing over.
1	lg	Egg, beaten	-Roll steak jelly roll fashion.
1		Flank steak	-Tie with kitchen twine.
1	tbs	Butter	-Lightly flour steak roll.
1	tbs	Oil	-Brown in butter and oil.
1	cup	Beef stock	-Add stock and red wine.
1	cup	Red wine	-Cover and simmer for two hours.
1	recipe	Oyster sauce	-Slice steak and garnish with Oyster Sauce.

SAUCE D'HUITRES

OYSTER SAUCE

1	pt	Oysters and their liquid	-Drain oysters reserving 1 cup of their liquid.
2	tbs	Butter	-Saute oysters in butter until their edges curl.
1/4	cup	Flour	-Make a roux with flour and butter.
1/4	cup	Butter	-Add cream and oyster liquid.
1	cup	Cream	-Wisk until lightly thickened.
1/8	tsp	Red pepper	-Add oysters and butter.
1/8	tsp	Black pepper	-Season with peppers.

BOEUF AUX OLIVES

BEEF AND OLIVES IN RED WINE SAUCE

A colorful and tasty dish combines tender beef, bell pepper and olives in a red wine sauce.

2	lbs	Beef tenderloin or other tender cut	
1	lg	Onion, chopped	
2		Bell peppers, red if possible	
1/2	tsp	Herbes de Provence	
1	clove	Garlic, crushed	
		Salt and pepper	
1	cup	Dry red wine	
1	cup	Green olives, pimiento stuffed	

-Saute the diced beef in the butter on high heat for about 5 minutes.
-Remove beef, drain and keep warm.
-Saute onions in the same skillet about 2 minutes.
-Add bell pepper and mix well.
-Cook about 10 minutes on medium heat.
-Add herbes de Provence, garlic, salt and pepper.
-Pour in the wine.
-Cover and simmer 10 minutes.
-Add the reserved beef and the green olives.
-Cook another 10 minutes.
-Garnish with parsley.

BOULETTES DE VIANDE A L'ITALIENNE

VEAL MEAT BALLS ITALIAN STYLE

Veal and sausage meat balls are combined with wide egg noodles and aromatic vegetables bound together with a rich sauce.

1		Onion, chopped
1	tbs	Butter
1	tbs	Oil
1 1/2	lbs	Ground veal
2/3	lb	Sausage, bulk
1/4	tsp	Marjoram
		Salt and pepper
		Flour for dredging
3	tbs	Butter
3	tbs	Oil
3		Onions, sliced
3	stalks	Celery, sliced
2		Bell peppers, red or green, sliced
1/2	lb	Mushrooms, sliced
1/2	cup	White wine
1	cup	Beef stock
4	tbs	Tomato paste
		Salt and pepper
1/2	lb	Egg noodles, wide
3	tbs	Parmesan cheese
1/2	cup	Swiss cheese, grated

-Saute the chopped onion in butter and oil for two minutes.
-Add the sausage and cook about 5 minutes.
-Remove sausage to a bowl with veal, marjoram, salt and pepper.
-Mix well and prepare meat balls.
-Roll in flour.
-Saute meat balls in butter and oil about 5 to 6 minutes.
-Remove and keep warm.
-Saute the onions, celery, peppers and mushrooms in the same skillet about 5 minutes.
-Add the wine, stock, tomato paste, salt and pepper.
-Simmer about 15 minutes.
-Add the cooked noodles to the meatballs.
-Add the vegetables and sauce and mix gently.
-Add the parmeasan.
-Mix gently.
-Sprinkle with Swiss cheese.
-Place in a 350 degree oven for 10 minutes

BOEUF AU POIVRON ET AUX CHAMPIGNONS

BRAISED BEEF, PEPPERS AND MUSHROOMS

Beef, peppers and mushrooms braise slowly for 2 1/2 hours in wine and stock for a hardy meal. Serve with noodles.

2	lbs	Beef -chuck, round or rump- cut in 1 inch cubes	-Place the beef in a large bowl.
1		Onion, chopped	-Add the onions, thyme, rosemary, parsley, cayenne, bay leaf, wine and olive oil.
1	tsp	Thyme	-Mix well, cover and marinate three hours.
1	tsp	Rosemary	-Saute the onions, mushrooms and peppers in butter and oil about 8 minutes on high heat.
1	tsp	Parsley	
1/8	tsp	Cayenne	
1		Bay leaf	-Remove vegetables and set aside.
1	cup	Red wine	-Drain the beef reserving marinade.
1	cup	Beef stock	-Saute in same skillet until lightly brown.
2	tbs	Olive oil	-Add flour, reduce heat and cook for 2 minutes.
2		Onions, sliced.	
1/2	lb	Mushrooms, whole	-Add marinade and stock.
2		Bell pepper, sliced	-Bring to a boil.
1	tbs	Butter	-Cover and simmer 1 1/2 hours.
1	tsp	Oil	-Add the reserved vegetables.
2	tbs	Flour	-Cover and cook another hour.

> **To BRAISE means to cook in a covered pot such as a dutch oven with a small amount of liquid, slowly for a long period of time. Usually used for tougher cuts of meat or older fowl. It is a moist heat type of cooking which can be done on top of the stove or in the oven.**

RAGOUT DE BOEUF A LA GRECQUE

BEEF STEW GREEK STYLE

This traditional Greek dish called STIFADO is interesting for its combination of spices and the final garnish of feta cheese.

3 1/2	lbs	Sirloin tip, cut into 3/4 inch cubes	-Dredge the beef cubes in flour.
		Flour for dredging	-Saute in butter and oil until golden.
3	tbs	Butter	-Place beef in an oven proof casserole.
3	tbs	Oil	-Add to the skillet the stock, tomato paste, vinegar, cinnamon stick, thyme, cumin, salt and pepper.
2	cups	Beef stock	
3	tbs	Tomato paste	
3	tbs	Tarragon vinegar	-Bring to a boil.
1	stick	Cinnamon	-Pour over the beef.
1	tsp	Thyme	-Cover and cook in a 350 degree oven for 2 1/2 hours.
1/2	tsp	Cumin	
		Salt and pepper	-Add onions the last 30 minutes of the cooking.
1	lb	Boiling onions (small)	
1/3	lb	Feta cheese	-Uncover and add the feta cheese the last 2 minutes.
1	tbs	Parsley, chopped	

HACHIS PARMENTIER

BEEF AND POTATOES AU GRATIN

Named after the man who popularized the American potato in France and Europe this ground beef casserole is topped with cheese flavored potatoes.

2		Onions, chopped	
1	cup	Celery, chopped	
2	tbs	Butter	
2	tbs	Oil	
2	lbs	Ground beef	
1	lb	Tomatoes, peeled, seeded and chopped	
1/2	tsp	Thyme	
1/4	tsp	Quatre-epices	
1/2	lb	Carrots, peeled and chopped	
		Salt and pepper	
2	lbs	Potatoes, peeled and boiled	
3		Eggs	
1	cup	Milk	
		Salt and pepper	
1/2	cup	Swiss cheese, grated	

-Saute onions and celery in butter and oil about 3 to 4 minutes.
-Add the ground beef stirring well.
-Add the tomatoes, thyme, quatre-epices, carrots, salt and pepper.
-Mix well and cook about 15 minutes on a high heat.
-Rice or mash the potatoes.
-Add eggs, milk, salt, pepper and cheese.
-Place meat mixture in a baking dish.
-With the aid of a pastry bag pipe out potato mixture on top in a decorative manner; covering the whole dish.
-Bake in a 400 degree oven for 30 minutes.

CROQUETTES DE BOEUF EN SAUCE TOMATE

BEEF CROQUETTES IN TOMATO SAUCE

We are all familiar with salmon or chicken croquettes but beef croquettes are unusual. Prepared here with a tomato sauce on a bed of rice and garnished with sour cream, they are delicious.

1 1/2	lbs	Ground beef	
1	lg	Onion, chopped	
1/4	tsp	Quatre-epices	
1/8	tsp	Cayenne	
		Salt and pepper	
1		Egg, beaten	
1	cup	Flour for dredging	
2		Eggs, beaten	
1	cup	Bread crumbs	
10	oz	Tomato sauce	
1/2	tsp	Marjoram	
8	cups	Cooked rice	
1/2	cup	Sour cream	

-Mix well the ground beef, onions, quatre epices, cayenne, salt, pepper and egg.
-Form eight croquettes in oval shapes.
-Pass each croquette in flour then in egg and finally in bread crumbs.
-Saute the croquettes in butter and oil about 2 minutes on each side.
-Add the tomato sauce and marjoram.
-Cover and cook 5 minutes.
-Remove the croquettes and keep warm.
-Raise heat and reduce sauce about 10 minutes.
-Serve the croquettes on a bed of rice, topped with some of the sauce and garnished with a tablespoon of sour cream.

HAMBURGERS A LA CREME D'OIGNONS

HAMBURGERS WITH CREAMED ONIONS

Well seasoned ground beef hamburgers sauteed to perfection rest on bed of smothered onions for a taste of your life.

2 1/2	lbs	Onions, cut in rings
2	tbs	Butter
2	tbs	Oil
6	tbs	Beef stock
2	lbs	Ground beef
3	cloves	Garlic, chopped
1	tsp	Quatre-epices
1/8	tsp	Cayenne
1 1/2	tsp	Anchovy paste.
		Salt and pepper
1/8	tsp	Nutmeg
3	tbs	Vinegar
6	sm	Sweet pickles, chopped

-Saute the onions in butter and oil about 5 minutes.
-Add beef stock mixing well.
-Cover and cook slowly for 20 minutes, stirring from time to time.
-Blend the ground steak, garlic, quatre epices, cayenne, anchovy paste, salt, pepper and nutmeg.
-Form into equal size hamburgers.
-Saute the hamburgers for 4 to 5 minutes on each side.
-Remove and keep warm.
-Add salt and the vinegar to the onions.
-Let vinegar evaporate.
-Arrange onions on a serving platter.
-Place steaks over the onions.
-Garnish with chopped sweet pickles.

PORK

COTE DE PORC AUX CERISES

PORK CHOPS WITH CHERRIES

Fruit and pork seem to have a natural affinity to each other as is illustrated in this recipe.

8		Boneless pork chops 1 inch thick	-Salt and pepper chops.
		Salt and pepper	-Saute chops about 3 minutes on both sides in
1	tbs	Oil	butter and oil.
1	tbs	Butter	-Drain fat from pan.
1	oz	Kirsch, heated	-Pour heated Kirsch over and flame.
1/2	cup	Beef stock	-Add stock.
1	l-lb	Can pitted, dark cherries	-Cover and simmer 1 hour.
1/2	tsp	Nutmeg	-Add nutmeg, cloves, marjoram and lemon
1/2	tsp	Cloves	zest to syrup.
1/2	tsp	Marjoram	-Blend lemon juice and cornstarch.
1/2	tsp	Lemon zest	-Add the syrup mixture.
2	tbs	Lemon juice	-Cook until thick.
2	tsp	Cornstarch	-Add bovril.
1	tsp	Bovril	-After chops have cooked 45 minutes add
			syrup mixture.
			-Add cherries the last 2 minutes.

DAUBE DE PORC AUX POIVRONS

BRAISED PORK AND PEPPERS WITH NOODLES

Tender pieces of pork and crunchy bell peppers are combined with noodles and a light orange sauce.

1	lg	Onion, chopped	-Saute the onions in butter and oil for 2 or 3
1	tbs	Butter	minutes.
1	tbs	Oil	-Add the pork cubes.
2	lbs	Pork filets cut into 1/2 inch cubes	-When pork is brown add the flour.
1	tbs	Flour	-Cook for 1 minute
1	cup	Chicken stock	-Add the stock, soy sauce, orange juice and
1	tbs	Soy sauce	tabasco.
1/2	cup	Orange juice	-Cover and simmer 1 hour.
3	drops	Tabasco	-Add the peppers and the cooked noodles.
2	lg	Green peppers, sliced thinly	-Cook 10 minutes more turning frequently.
1/3	lb	Thin egg noodles, cooked	

COTE DE PORC SAUCE DIABLE

SAUTEED PORK FILETS-DEVIL SAUCE

Devilishly good are these chops garnished with a vinegar, mustard and sour cream sauce with sweet pickles for a contrasting taste.

6	3/4 in	Loin pork chops, bone removed	-Flatten chops between wax paper.
		Flour	-Dredge in salted flour.
3	tbs	Butter	-Brown chops in butter and oil.
1	tbs	Oil	-Remove and keep warm loosely covered in a
		Salt and pepper	200 degree oven.
2	tbs	Vinegar	-Add vinegar and stock to pan and deglaze
1	cup	Chicken stock	pan.
1	cup	Sour cream	-Reduce sauce by one third.
2	tbs	Dijon mustard	-Off fire add sour cream and mustard.
1	tbs	Green peppercorns	-Wisk over low heat.
		Small sweet pickles	-Add peppercorns.
			-Cook slowly until sauce thickens.
			-Pour over chops.
			-Garnish with sweet pickles.

DEGLAZE is the technique of loosening all the cooking juices in a pan, after it has been DEGREASED, by pouring a liquid stock, wine, other cooking liquid in the hot skillet to capture all the concentrated flavors. The resulting liquid is usually used to make a sauce to accompany the food cooked.

COTE DE PORC AUX POMMES

PORK CHOPS WITH APPLES

Quick and easy pork chops and apples are braised and a mustard sauce is created from the braising liquid. Serve with boiled noodles.

6		Pork chops	-Saute the chops in butter and oil for 3
		Salt and pepper	minutes on each side.
4		Apples, peeled and cut into thin	-Salt and pepper.
		slices	-Cover with the apples.
3/4	cup	Chicken stock	-Add the stock.
3	tbs	Dijon mustard	-Cover and simmer for 20 minutes.
			-Remove the chops and apples to a serving dish.
			-Keep warm.
			-Reduce the pan juices for 5 minutes.
			-Add the mustard blending well.
			-Pour sauce over the chops and apples.

ROTI DE PORC EN COURONNE

CROWN ROAST OF PORK

On our special one hour Christmas show, we prepared this crown roast and stuffed the center with cranberry, pecan and rice dressing. A sight to behold.

2		Pork loins, center cuts, 8-9 ribs each backbone removed
6	cloves	Garlic
		Butter, softened
		Salt and pepper
1/2	tsp	Rosemary leaves, crushed
1	recipe	Cranberry, Pecan, Rice Stuffing

-Cut a 1 inch slit between each rib where the backbone was removed.
-Make three slits in each rib in the meaty parts.
-Place a clove of garlic in each slit.
-Tie the two loins together, bone side in with kitchen string to form a circle.
-Trim between and around each rib about 1 inch down the bone.
-Save the trimmings for stuffing.
-Place in a baking pan.
-Rub all over with softened butter.
-Salt and pepper.
-Sprinkle with rosemary.
-Place in a preheated oven and bake at 350 degrees for 25 minutes per pound (meat thermometer 165 degrees).
-Remove from oven.
-Fill with stuffing.
-Return to oven for another 15-20 minutes.
-Remove from oven again.
-Let rest for 15 minutes before serving.

FARCIS DES CANNEBERGES, NOIX ET RIZ

CRANBERRY, PECAN, RICE STUFFING

1/2	cup	Raisins
1/4	cup	White wine
1	cup	Onions, chopped
1	cup	Celery, chopped
2	cups	Apples, cubed
1 1/2	cup	Cranberries
2	cloves	Garlic
1/2	cup	Parsley, chopped
1/2	tsp	Thyme
1/4	tsp	Mace
1/4	tsp	Sage
		Salt and pepper
1	cup	Pecans, toasted
2	cups	Wild rice, cooked
2	cups	Brown rice, cooked

-Soak raisins in wine for 30 minutes.
-Saute pork trimmings from above recipe.
-Add onions and saute for 3 minutes.
-Add celery, apples, cranberries, garlic, parsley, raisins and wine.
-Heat through.
-Add thyme, mace, sage, salt and pepper.
-Add pecans.
-Blend well.
-Mix with wild and brown rice.
-Use to fill crown of pork roast or put into a casserole and bake for 15 minutes at 350 degrees.

ESCALOPES DE PORK GRATINEES

PORK AND MUSHROOMS GRATIN

Pork and mushrooms are covered with a lemon, wine and cream sauce, topped with Swiss cheese and browned in the oven.

8		Pork filets, thin
1	tbs	Butter
1	tbs	Oil
		Salt and pepper
1	lb	Mushrooms
4	tbs	Lemon juice
4	tbs	Vermouth
1/2	cup	Cream
		Salt and pepper
1/8	tsp	Nutmeg
1/3	cup	Swiss cheese

-Saute the pork filets in butter and oil for 4 minutes on each side.
-Remove to an oven proof dish and keep warm.
-Salt and pepper.
-Saute the mushrooms in the same skillet until their liquid evaporates.
-Place over the pork.
-Discard all the fat.
-Add the lemon juice and vermouth.
-Deglace the pan.
-Add cream.
-Reduce by half.
-Salt and pepper.
-Add nutmeg.
-Pour over mushrooms.
-Sprinkle with cheese.
-Place in a 500 degree oven for 5 to 6 minutes to brown cheese.

Mushrooms are very pourus and will absorb moisture readily. They should not be washed in lots of water. Wipe each mushroom with a damp cloth or papertowel.

CHOU FARCI A LA NICOISE

STUFFED CABBAGE NICOISE

Cabbage leaves, a savory stuffing of sausage, tomato, rice and green peas are reformed into a head and then braised in stock. It is then served with a tomato sauce and a little sour cream. Good!

1		Cabbage, 3 1/2 lbs
		Salt
1/3	lb	Bacon, diced
2		Onions, chopped
1 1/2	lb	Sausage meat
2		Tomatoes, peeled and diced
1	cup	Green peas
2	cups	Rice, cooked
1	clove	Garlic
		Salt and pepper

-Remove the core from the cabbage.
-Cook 10 minutes in boiling salted water.
-Refresh in cold water.
-Drain.
-Fry bacon in a skillet.
-Add the onions and cook 5 minutes.
-Separate the cabbage leaves setting aside the large outer leaves.
-Chop the heart of the cabbage.
-Blend together the sausage, bacon, onions, tomatoes, rice, green peas, salt and pepper.
-Place a large piece of cheese cloth in a large mixing bowl.
-Line the bowl with cabbage leaves, stem ends up.
-Place 1 cup of stuffing in the bottom.
-Add a layer of chopped cabbage.
-Repeat sausage, cabbage layers until all is used.
-Fold stem ends over stuffing.
-Add additional leaves to cover stuffing.
-Bring cheese cloth up together and tie with kitchen string.
-Place in boiling stock and simmer for 2 1/2 to 3 hours.
-Remove from liquid.
-Drain and rest 5 minutes.
-Place on a serving platter.
-Surround with tomato sauce.
-Serve with sour cream on the side.

SAUCE TOMATE

TOMATO SAUCE

1		Onion, chopped
3		Tomatoes, peeled and seeded
1/4	tsp	Thyme
		Salt and pepper
16	oz	Tomato sauce

-Saute onions in a little oil.
-Chop tomatoes and add to onions.
-Season with thyme, salt and pepper.
-Add tomato sauce.
-Simmer 15 to 20 minutes.

TRANCHES DE JAMBON ROULE AUX PECHES

HAM ROLLS WITH PEACHES

An unusual stuffing combines peaches, onions, cinnamon and bread, rolled in ham slices, covered with peach halves and baked for a new way to serve ham.

24	oz	Peach halves, canned
30		Cloves, whole
4		Green onions, chopped
1/8	tsp	Cinnamon
2	oz	Bread crumbs
2	tbs	Parsley, chopped
		Salt and pepper
6	slices	Ham, cut thin
6	tbs	Lemon juice
1	tbs	Sugar
1	tbs	Dijon mustard

-Drain peaches and save 3/4 cup of juice.
-Place 5 cloves in each of 6 peach halves and set aside.
-Chop the rest of the peaches and place in a bowl.
-Add the green onions, cinnamon, bread crumbs and parsley.
-Salt and pepper to taste.
-Blend well.
-On each slice of ham place 1/6 of the peach mixture.
-Roll each slice to enclose.
-Secure with a toothpick.
-Place in a buttered baking dish.
-Blend together the reserved peach juice, lemon juice, sugar and mustard.
-Pour over ham rolls.
-Place in a 300 degree oven for 40 minutes.
-Baste the ham rolls.
-Place the peach halves over ham rolls.
-Return to the oven for 10 minutes.
-Arrange ham rolls on a serving platter.
-Surround with peaches.
-Pour pan juices over ham.
-Garnish with watercress.

BEIGNETS DE JAMBON

HAM AND CHEESE FRITTERS

These deep fried beignets or fritters are delicious. Be prepared to make many.

2	lg	Potatoes, grated
1	lg	Onion, chopped
1	lb	Ham, chopped
2		Eggs, beaten
1/2	cup	Swiss cheese
8	tbs	Flour
2	tsp	Baking powder
		Salt and pepper
		Oil for frying

-Blend together the grated potatoes, onion, ham, eggs, cheese, flour, baking powder, salt and pepper.
-Heat 1 inch oil in a deep frying pan.
-Laddle the ham mixture (1/4 cup at a time) into the oil.
-Let them swell and brown 7 minutes on each side.
-Remove to absorbent paper.

TRANCHES DE JAMBON FINES BOUCHES

HAM STEAKS GOURMET

Thick ham slices sauteed in butter placed on a bed of spinach and garnished with a sauce made with madeira wine, brandy, beef stock and cream becomes gourmet ham.

3	lbs	Ham steak, 1/2 inch thick
2	tbs	Butter
1	tbs	Peanut oil
3	tbs	Flour
1/2	cup	Green onion, chopped
1	cup	Beef stock
1/2	cup	Madeira wine
1	tbs	Tomato paste
		Black pepper
1 1/2	cup	Heavy cream
3	tbs	Brandy
4	cups	Chopped spinach, cooked and drained

-Trim ham and cut into serving size.
-Brown lightly in butter and oil.
-Set aside.
-Add flour to pan blending well.
-Add green onions.
-Add beef stock and madeira wine.
-Add tomato paste and pepper.
-Blend in the cream.
-Simmer 4 to 5 minutes.
-Add brandy.
-Return ham slices to sauce.
-Heat spinach with a little butter.
-Spread spinach on a serving dish.
-Place ham slices over spinach.
-Spoon sauce over ham.

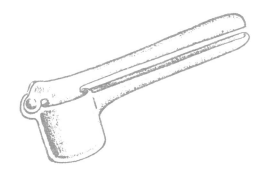

GIDOT D'AGNEAU FARCI AUX ABRICOTS

LEG OF LAMB STUFFED WITH APRICOTS

Our one hour special Easter show featured this boned leg of lamb which was stuffed with a rice dressing flavored with apricots, lemon zest and mint. It was delicious.

5	lb	Leg of lamb, deboned
1	cup	Dried apricots
1	lg	Onion, chopped
2	tbs	Peanut oil
		Zest of one lemon
2	tbs	Parsley, chopped
1	tbs	Mint leaves, chopped
1/4	tsp	Quatre-espices*
1 1/2	cups	Cooked rice
		Salt and pepper
1		Egg
3	tbs	Butter
1/2	cup	Beef broth
1	tbs	Cornstarch
3	tbs	Cold water
		Mint sprigs or watercress for garnish

-Soak the apricots in water to cover.
-Cook for 10 minutes.
-Drain and reserve 1 cup of liquid.
-Chop apricots and set side.
-Saute onions in oil.
-Add lemon zest, parsley, spices, rice and apricots.
-Salt and pepper.
-Add the egg and blend well.
-Place stuffing on the inside of the boned leg of lamb.
-Tie with kitchen string.
-Butter a baking pan and place leg in it.
-Bake in a 425 degree oven about two hours, basting frequently.
-In the same skillet you made the stuffing, melt the rest of the butter.
-Add the apricot boiling water.
-Add the beef stock.
-Salt and pepper.
-Add the cornstarch blended with the water.
-Bring to a boil.
-Place leg on a serving dish.
-Dab with some of the sauce.
-Serve rest of sauce along side.
-Garnish meat with sprigs of mint or watercress.

Quatre-epices: A mixture of four spices common in France. Usually a mixture of pepper, ground cloves, ground ginger or cinnamon and ground nutmeg. Blend equal parts to taste.

To REDUCE is the technique of boiling a liquid rapidly to reduce its quantity. The result is a thicker liquid with a highly concentrated flavor. An important step in making many sauces especially where the liquid is the result of DEGLAZING a cooking vessel.

To cut firm butter into neat slices heat knife blade in hot water for each cut or cover blade with waxed paper.

Partially freeze raw meat or chicken breasts for ease in cutting.

Poultry

POULTRY

POULET A LA DUCHESS
    CHICKEN ALMA PEYROUX

POULET MARINE FRIT
    MARINATED FRIED CHICKEN

SUPREME DE VOLAILLE A LA MARSALA
    BREAST OF CHICKEN MARSALA

POULET UN, DEUX, TROIS
    CHICKEN ONE, TWO, THREE

SAUCE UN, DEUX, TROIS
    SAUCE ONE, TWO, THREE

SUPREMES DE VOLAILLES QUARTRE SAISONS
    SAUTEED CHICKEN BREASTS FOUR SEASONS

BLANC DE VOLAILLE MEDITERRANEE
    CHICKEN BREASTS MEDITERRANEAN

POULET SAUTE AU WISKEY
    DRUNK CHICKEN

POULET EN CASSEROLE
    CHICKEN SUPREME

POULET EN BROCHETTE AUX BEURRE ANCHOIS
    SKEWERED CHICKEN-ANCHOVY BUTTER

POULET AUX PAPRIKA
    CHICKEN PAPRIKA

POULET SAUCE PIQUANT
    CHICKEN SAUCE PIQUANT

FRICASSEE DE VOLAILLES AU VINAIGRE DE VIN
    CHICKEN IN RED WINE AND VINEGAR

POULET CHOSSEUR
CHICKEN CHOSSEUR

POULET AU NOIX
CHICKEN PECANDINE

SUPREME DE VOLAILLE EN CROUTE
CHICKEN BAKED WITH MUSHROOM SAUCE IN FILO

JAMBONETTES DE VOLAILLE
STUFFED CHICKEN LEGS

POULET A LA TETRAZZINI
CHICKEN TETRAZZINI

BALLOTTINE DE POULET
STUFFED WHOLE CHICKEN

FARCI
STUFFING

ESCALOPES DE DINDE AU FOUR
BAKED TURKEY SCALLOPS

DINDE AU FOUR
BAKED TURKEY

PAIN DE MAIS FARCI
CORN BREAD DRESSING

PAIN DE MAIS
CORN BREAD

SAUCE AUX GESIERS
GIBLET GRAVY

POULTRY

It is difficult for me to say what is my favorite food since there is hardly any reasonable food product that I do not enjoy. However, poultry is high on my list of most favorites. I believe its because it lends itself to so many variations.

In this chapter we add some interesting recipes to the 45 that are in Volume I. We fry, bake, saute, braise the bird in all its parts. We flavor it with herbs, spices, wine, nuts, vegetables, vinegar and even whiskey.

We begin this chapter with a very old recipe taught to my mother by my great grandmother (and who knows who taught her). This one is well over 120 years old. For lack of a proper name I called it Poulet a la Duchess in memory of my mother (Duchess was her nickname.) I guarantee you will enjoy this one, especially the potatoes.

POULET A LA DUCHESS

CHICKEN ALMA PEYROUX

A very old specialty of my mother was this unusual French way of cooking chicken. All skin is removed from the chicken which is then seasoned. As it is fried it is placed into a dutch oven. The potatoes are then fried in the same oil and added to the chicken along with chopped parsley and garlic. The chicken is good but the potatoes are delicious.

3		Chickens, cut for frying
		Peanut oil for frying
6	lbs	Potatoes, peeled and cut for french frying
3	cloves	Garlic, chopped
1/2	cup	Parsley, chopped
		Salt and pepper

-Remove the skin from chicken pieces (except wings).
-Salt and pepper each piece.
-Heat peanut oil in a large skillet.
-Fry chicken first.
-Fry potatoes in the same oil.
-As chicken and potatoes are cooked, place them in a large dutch oven over low heat.
-Sprinkle with garlic and parsley.
-Cover.
-Let rest for 10 minutes, covered.
-Arrange chicken and potatoes on serving plate.

POULET MARINE FRIT

MARINATED FRIED CHICKEN

A bouquet of seven aromatic herbs, lemon juice and olive oil marinate chicken pieces before the anglaise coating is applied. When fried, it provides a great taste experience.

1 1/2		Chickens, cut into 12 or more serving pieces	
		Salt and pepper	
2		Lemons	
2	tbs	Parsley, chopped	
1	tsp	Chevril	
1/2	tsp	Tarragon	
1	tsp	Chives	
1/2	tsp	Thyme	
1/2	tsp	Basil	
1/4	tsp	Rosemary	
1/2	cup	Olive oil	
1	cup	Flour in a bowl	
3		Eggs, beaten in a bowl	
2	cups	Bread crumbs in a bowl	
		Oil for frying	
1	cup	Mayonnaise	
2	tbs	Dijon mustard	
1	clove	Garlic, chopped	

-Salt and pepper the chicken.
-Place in a baking dish.
-Squeeze one lemon over the chicken.
-Blend together the parsley, chevril, tarragon, chives, thyme, basil and rosemary.
-Blend with the olive oil.
-Pour over the chicken and marinate 3 hours, turning frequently.
-Roll each piece of chicken in flour.
-Pass in the egg.
-Then roll in bread crumbs.
-Heat about one inch of oil in a heavy skillet.
-Place chicken in oil.
-Fry about 10-12 minutes on one side.
-Turn and fry another 10-12 minutes.
-Mix the mayonnaise, mustard and garlic together.
-Serve chicken with the mayonnaise sauce on the side.

SUPREME DE VOLAILLE A LA MARSALA

BREAST OF CHICKEN MARSALA

Tender chicken breasts coated with bread crumbs are sauteed in butter and a wonderful sauce is made with Marsala wine. Mushrooms cooked in the sauce garnish the chicken.

8		Chicken breasts, skinned and boned
1	cup	Flour
2		Eggs, beaten
2	cups	Bread crumbs
2	tbs	Butter
1	tbs	Peanut oil
1/2	lb	Mushrooms
2	tbs	Flour
1/2	cup	Marsala wine, dry
1	clove	Garlic, minced
3/4	cup	Chicken broth
1	lemon	Sliced
		Salt and pepper

-Dredge chicken in flour.
-Dip in beaten egg.
-Coat with bread crumbs.
-Saute breasts in butter and oil on both sides until golden.
-Remove to serving platter.
-Add mushrooms to saute pan and cook about one minute.
-Sprinkle 2 tbs flour over mushrooms.
-Cook about 30 seconds.
-Add marsala, garlic, chicken broth and lemon slices.
-Cook until thickened.
-Salt and pepper to taste.
-Pour over chicken.

POULET UN, DEUX, TROIS

CHICKEN ONE, TWO, THREE

Chicken one, two, three was a recipe provided by Kathy Kasta of Cooking Good Chickens on the occasion of a field trip to their farm in Defuniac Springs, Florida, for show 167.

6		Chicken breast halves, deboned
2	cups	Mushrooms, sliced
1	cup	Scallions, sliced
1/2	cup	Mozzarella cheese, grated
4	tbs	Butter cut into 6 fingers, chilled
3/4	cup	Flour
2		Eggs, beaten
3/4	cup	Bread crumbs, unseasoned
		Butter for sauteeing, clarified

-Saute mushrooms and scallions in a little butter.
-Flatten the chicken breasts between sheets of waxed paper.
-Place a finger of butter in center of chicken.
-Place equal parts of the mushroom/scallion mixture and the cheese on the chicken.
-Roll up chicken and secure with tooth picks.
-Dust each roll with flour.
-Dip in beaten egg.
-Roll in bread crumbs.
-Saute the chicken rolls in the clarified butter turning frequently until brown and crispy, about 20 minutes.
-Or bake in a 350 degree oven for 45 minutes to 1 hour.

SAUCE UN, DEUX, TROIS

SAUCE ONE, TWO, THREE

2	tbs	Wine vinegar
2	tbs	Dijon mustard
1	cup	Cream
8	oz	Spinach noodles, cooked

-Over very high heat, deglaze the skillet in which the POULET UN, DEUX, TROIS was prepared with the wine vinegar.
-Add dijon mustard and blend well.
-Add the cream and cook until thickened (2 3 minutes).
-Pour over boiled spinach noodles.

To SAUTE is that cooking technique whereby food is cooked in a small amount of fat in an open skillet. The fat should be hot, the food dry and the food should not crowd the pan. In SAUTEEING the food, which can be coated or uncoated, should brown and create a crust quickly sealing in the natural juices.

SUPREMES DE VOLAILLES QUARTRE SAISONS
SAUTEED CHICKEN BREASTS FOUR SEASONS

Chicken supremes are coated with flour, eggs and pasta then sauteed in butter. The pasta becomes crispy.

1	lb	Spinach	-Cook and drain spinach.
		Salt and pepper	-Squeeze dry.
1/4	tsp	Nutmeg	-Cut each chicken breast in half lengthwise.
1	tbs	Olive oil	-Season with salt, pepper and olive oil.
4	oz	Butter	-Pound between wax paper.
6		Green onions, chopped	-Melt butter in a skillet.
1/2	lb	Mushrooms, sliced	-Saute green onions.
		Juice of 1/2 lemon	-Add mushrooms and saute until done.
3		Eggs, beaten	-Add spinach, lemon juice, salt, pepper and
2	tbs	Parmesan cheese	nutmeg.
1	cup	Vermicelli, cooked and cut into small pieces	-Cook until liquid is absorbed.
		Flour for dredging	-Keep warm.
			-Blend eggs and cheese.
6		Chicken breasts, skinned and boned	-Fold vermicelli into egg mixture.
8	oz	Butter, clarified	-Dredge chicken pieces in the flour, then in the egg mixture.
		Tomato slices for garnish	-Saute in clarified butter until crisp and golden.
			-Arrange spinach on a serving platter.
			-Top with chicken breasts.
			-Garnish platter with tomato slices.

BLANC DE VOLAILLE MEDITERRANEE
CHICKEN BREASTS MEDITERRANEAN

Thin chicken breasts breaded and sauteed are garnished with a light tomato sauce enriched with onions, mushrooms, garlic and black olives. Chicken and sauce are served over a bed of thin pasta.

6		Chicken breast halves deboned	-Pound the chicken breasts lightly between wax paper.
2	tbs	Flour	-Salt and pepper to taste.
		Salt and pepper	-Dredge in flour lightly.
2	tbs	Butter	-Heat butter and oil in a skillet.
2	tbs	Peanut oil	-Saute chicken about 3 minutes on each side.
2	cloves	Garlic, minced	-Remove and keep warm.
1	cup	Onion, chopped	-In the same skillet saute the onions, garlic
1/2	lb	Mushrooms, sliced	and mushrooms.
2	cups	Tomatoes, peeled and seeded	-Add tomatoes.
1/2	cup	White wine	-Pour in the wine and stock.
1/2	cup	Chicken stock	-Place chicken breasts in sauce.
1/2	cup	Black olives, pitted and sliced	-Lower heat to simmer.
1/3	cup	Parsley, chopped	-Cook about five minutes.
1	lb	Vermecelli, cooked according to the package directions	-Add olives and heat through (1 minute).
			-Cover a large serving dish with pasta.
			-Arrange chicken breasts over pasta.
			-Pour sauce over the chicken.
			-Garnish with parsley.

POULET SAUTE AU WISKEY

DRUNK CHICKEN

Sauteed chicken and mushrooms are braised in chicken stock and bourbon whiskey producing a delicious sauce, especially good with boiled noodles.

3	lb	Broiler-fryer, cut up
		Salt
		Pepper
1/4	cup	Butter
1	lb	Mushrooms finely sliced
1/2	cup	Bourbon
1/3	cup	Chicken broth
2	tbs	Tomato paste
1/4	tsp	Worchestershire sauce
1	tbs	Flour
1	tbs	Butter, soft
4	oz	Pimientos, drained and cut in 1/4-inch-wide strips

-Sprinkle chicken pieces with salt and pepper.
-Heat 1/4 cup butter in large skillet over medium heat.
-Brown chicken pieces on all sides. Remove. Reserve.
-Add mushrooms to fat left in skillet.
-Cook 2 to 3 minutes, stirring occasionally.
-Return chicken pieces to skillet.
-Add bourbon, chicken broth, tomato paste and Worchestershire.
-Cover.
-Bring to boiling.
-Simmer 15 to 20 minutes or until chicken is tender.
-Arrange chicken pieces in serving dish.
-Blend flour and 1 tablespoon softened butter until smooth.
-Add mixture to sauce; cook, stirring constantly, until thickened.
-Add pimientos.
-Stir in gently.
-Cook 1 minute.
-Correct seasoning of sauce to taste.
-Pour over chicken.

POULET EN CASSEROLE

CHICKEN SUPREME

Chicken, ham and mushrooms are baked in a casserole with a wine and sour cream topping. Delicious with noodles.

4		Chicken breasts (8 pieces), skinned and boned
1/3	cup	Flour
2	tsp	Salt
1	tsp	Paprika
1/4	cup	Butter
6		Slices boiled ham
1	tsp	Savory
		Celery leaves
1	cup	Mushrooms
1/2	cup	Dry white wine
1	cup	Sour cream

-Combine flour, salt and paprika in a paper bag.
-Place chicken in bag and shake to coat.
-Brown chicken lightly in butter.
-Place ham in bottom of a casserole.
-Sprinkle savory and celery leaves over ham.
-Place chicken over ham.
-Cover with mushrooms.
-Pour wine into skillet in which chicken was sauteed and stir well.
-Add remainder of seasoned flour to sour cream then blend into drippings.
-Pour over chicken.
-Cover and bake at 350 degrees for 1 hour.
-Serve with rice or noodles.

POULET EN BROCHETTE AUX BEURRE ANCHOIS

SKEWERED CHICKEN-ANCHOVY BUTTER

Pieces of chicken and Italian ham are interspersed with bread cubes and bay leaves on a skewer, brushed with anchovy butter and baked. Delicious.

4		Chicken breasts
8	oz	Prosciutto (thickly sliced)
2		Slices Italian bread
		Black pepper
16		Bay leaves
12	tbs	Butter
12		Anchovy filets

-Place chicken breasts on cutting board and halve each one.
-Slice each half horizontally.
-Pound the slices thin.
-Cut Prosciutto into small squares.
-Quarter the bread slices.
-Place a piece of Proscuitto on each chicken slice.
-Rub with pepper.
-Roll up chicken breasts.
-Thread onto skewers with pieces of bread, bay leaves and Prosciutto.
-Place skewers in a pan.
-Brush with butter.
-Bake at 400 degrees for 20 minutes.
-Mash anchovies in remaining butter.
-Pour over chicken before serving.

POULET AUX PAPRIKA

CHICKEN PAPRIKA

The sweet and gently spicy flavor of Hungarian paprika blended with chicken stock becomes the braising liquid in which the chicken is cooked. The braising liquid is enriched with sour cream and capers. Delicious served over noodles or rice.

2		Chickens cut into serving pieces
6	tbs	Butter
3	large	Onions, sliced
2	large	Bell peppers, sliced
4	large	Tomatoes, sliced
1	cup	Chicken broth
1	bottle	Capers, drained
1	cup	Sour cream
3	tbs	Flour blended with 3 tbs. of soft butter (beurre manie)
1/4	cup	Sweet paprika

-Heat butter in a heavy pan.
-Stir in the onions and cook until golden.
-Add paprika and stir in well.
-Add chicken turning pieces until well coated with the onion-paprika mixture.
-Add green peppers, tomatoes and chicken broth.
-Cover and cook gently until chicken is tender about 45 minutes.
-Remove pieces of chicken to a warm platter.
-Strain sauce through a sieve into another saucepan.
-Thicken with the beurre manie.
-Add sour cream and capers and mix well.
-Add chicken pieces and reheat gently.
-Serve with rice or noodles.

POULET SAUCE PIQUANT

CHICKEN SAUCE PIQUANT

This variation of Shrimp Creole braises chicken parts in a rich tomato sauce with mushrooms and green peas. Served over rice it is Creole cooking at its best.

1	3-lb	Chicken, cut in serving pieces	-Saute chicken in butter and oil until browned.
3	tbs	Butter	-Set aside.
2	tbs	Peanut oil	-Brown flour in pan juices.
3	tbs	Flour	-Add onions and saute.
2	cups	Onions, chopped	-Add tomatoes and liquid.
3	cups	Tomatoes, canned	-Bring to a boil.
2	cups	Chicken stock	-Return chicken to pan.
		Salt and pepper	-Add salt and pepper.
2	cups	Green peas	-Add green peas and mushrooms.
2	cups	Mushrooms	-Cover and cook slowly for about 1 hour or until chicken is tender.
			-Serve with boiled rice.

The larger the bird the more flesh in proportion to the bone.

FRICASSEE DE VOLAILLES AU VINAIGRE DE VIN

CHICKEN IN RED WINE AND VINEGAR

Chicken parts sauteed in butter then braised in red wine and vinegar with green onions and tomatoes is served with spinach and a sauce made from the cooking liquids.

12		Chicken parts of your choice	-Salt and pepper chicken parts.
		Salt and pepper	-Saute chicken in butter and oil until browned.
4	tbs	Butter	-Halfway through the cooking add the green onions, tomatoes, wine and vinegar.
2	tbs	Oil	-Cook rapidly to reduce the liquid about a third.
6		Green onions, chopped	-Add the stock.
2		Tomatoes, peeled and diced	-Simmer about 20 minutes.
1	cup	Wine vinegar	-Remove chicken to a serving dish.
1	cup	Red wine	-Keep warm.
2	cups	Chicken stock	-Wisk in butter a little at a time.
4	tbs	Butter	-Pour over chicken.
1	lb	Spinach, cooked	-Surround chicken with spinach.
			-Salt and pepper to taste.
			-Pour over chicken.

POULET CHOSSEUR

CHICKEN CHOSSEUR

Chicken, mushrooms and tomatoes are braised in white wine and aromatic seasonings. Exellent served over rice.

3	lbs	Chicken parts
1/2	cup	Flour
1	tsp	Salt
1/2	tsp	Pepper
1/2		Thyme
1/4	cup	Butter
1/4	cup	Green onions, chopped
1/2	cup	Mushrooms, chopped
1/2	cup	Dry white wine
3/4	cup	Tomatoes
2	tbs	Parsley
1/4	tsp	Chevril

-Blend flour, salt, pepper and thyme.
-Dust chicken lightly with flour mixture.
-Saute chicken in butter until golden.
-Add green onions, mushrooms, wine, tomatoes, parsley, and chevril.
-Cover and simmer 1/2 hour.

POULET AUX NOIX

CHICKEN PECANDINE

Chicken braised in wine flavored with lots of garlic cloves and aromatic herbs creates a wonderful sauce enriched with pecans. The garlic cloves which are well cooked are delicious when removed from their skins and spread on French bread.

3		Chickens, cut in serving pieces
4	oz	Bacon, cut in dice
4	tbs	Butter
2	tbs	Peanut oil
3		Onions, chopped
2	cups	Dry white wine
1	cup	Chicken stock
1		Bay leaf
4	sprigs	Parsley
1	tsp	Thyme
1/4	tsp	Rosemary
8		Green onions, chopped
10	cloves	Garlic, not peeled
		Salt and pepper
1	cup	Pecans

-In a large skillet, saute bacon until almost done.
-Add butter and oil.
-Saute chicken pieces until brown on all sides.
-Saute in two batches if necessary.
-Remove chicken to baking dish.
-Saute onions in skillet drippings.
-Deglaze the pan with the wine and stock.
-Bring to a boil and reduce five minutes.
-Make a bouquet garni of the bay leaf, parsley, thyme and rosemary.
-Add green onions, garlic cloves and bouquet garni to sauce.
-Salt and pepper the sauce.
-Pour over the chicken in the baking dish.
-Place in a 350 degree oven and bake for 20 minutes.
-Chop 2/3 of the pecans.
-Add to the sauce with the remaining 1/3 whole pecans.
-Cook another 20 minutes.
-Remove bouquet garni and garlic cloves.
-To serve, place the chicken on a serving dish.
-Pour some of the sauce over chicken and rest along side.
-Serve the garlic cloves along side.

NOTE: Walnuts can be substituted for the pecans.

SUPREME DE VOLAILLE EN CROUTE

CHICKEN BAKED WITH MUSHROOM SAUCE IN FILO

Delicious sauteed chicken breasts and mushrooms are wrapped in filo dough and baked to a flaky golden brown for this Greek style dish.

1/4	lb	Butter
1		Onion, chopped
1/2	lb	Mushrooms, chopped fine
2	tbs	Parsley, minced
1	clove	Garlic, minced
1 1/2	tbs	Flour
1/3	cup	Dry vermouth
		Salt and pepper
2	tbs	Vegetable oil
4		Chicken breast halves, skinned and boned
8		Filo leaves
1/2	cup	Melted butter
		Bread crumbs
1/3	cup	Pecans, chopped fine (optional)

-Saute onions in 3 tablespoons butter and set aside.
-Heat 3 tablespoons butter and heat mushrooms until juices evaporate.
-Add onions, parsley, garlic, pecans and saute.
-Stir in flour, mixing well and add vermouth.
-Stir over medium heat until thickened.
-Season with salt and pepper and set aside.
-In skillet, heat remaining butter and vegetable oil and saute breasts on each side (approximately 2 minutes on each side).
-Butter one sheet of filo and sprinkle with bread crumbs; cover with another sheet of filo and butter.
-Place chicken on filo.
-Put 1/4 of mushroom mixture on top and roll up.
-Butter outside well.
-Bake in a preheated oven at 350 degrees for 35 minutes or until golden brown.

JAMBONETTES DE VOLAILLE

STUFFED CHICKEN LEGS

Chicken legs and thighs are stuffed with chicken breast meat and livers sauteed with aromatic vegetables and seasonings then sauteed in butter. Deglazing the pan with red wine and reducing creates a rich sauce which is enriched with butter.

6		Chicken legs with thighs
2		Chicken breasts
2		Chicken livers
1	cup	Stale french bread
3/4	cup	Milk
2	tbs	Butter
1/2	cup	Onions, diced
3	cloves	Garlic, minced
1/4	cup	Parsley
1/2	tsp	Thyme
1/2	tsp	Sage
		Salt and pepper
6	tbs	Butter
3/4	cup	Red wine
1	tbs	Kitchen bouquet

-Debone chicken legs with thighs.
-Chop chicken breasts and livers finely.
-Soak bread with milk.
-Saute chicken breast and liver in butter.
-Add onions and saute until soft.
-Add garlic, parsley, thyme, sage, salt, pepper and milk soaked bread.
-Stuff chicken legs with mixture.
-Tie with kitchen string.
-Saute legs in 2 tbs butter until golden, about 10 minutes.
-Reduce heat and cover for 30 minutes.
-Remove chicken and keep warm.
-Add red wine to deglaze pan.
-Add kitchen bouquet.
-Reduce wine to 1/2 cup.
-Wisk in butter in small pieces over low heat.
-Add salt and pepper to taste.
-Remove string from chicken.
-Arrange on serving dish.
-Pour sauce over and around chicken.
-Garnish with chopped parsley.

A delicious casserole which blends boiled chicken, mushrooms, ham, pimiento and spaghettini bound together with a veloute sauce made with the boiling liquid and garnished with cheese is great for a crowd. Can be made with left over turkey.

4	cups	Water	-Bring water to a boil in a large stock pot.
1	cup	Onions, sliced	-Add onions, celery, carrot, thyme, bay
1/2	cup	Celery, chopped	leaves, salt and pepper.
1	tsp	Thyme	-Place chicken in the stock pot.
2		Bay leaves	-Simmer for 2 to 3 hours until chicken is
		Salt and pepper	tender.
1	cup	Mushrooms, sliced	-Remove chicken, cool and debone.
8	oz	Spaghettini	-Saute mushrooms in butter in a skillet and set
4	oz	Butter	aside.
1/2	cup	Flour	-Boil spaghettini until al dente.
8	oz	Butter	-Drain and return to pot with butter.
3	cups	Chicken stock	-Make a roux with the flour and butter.
2		Egg yolks	-Add stock and blend until thickened.
4	oz	Pimiento, chopped	-Blend in egg yolks.
1	cup	Ham, chopped	-Add mushrooms, pimiento, ham and
1/2	cup	Cheddar cheese	chicken.
1/4	cup	Parmesan cheese	-Place spaghettini in a large oven proof
			casserole.
			-Fold in chicken mixture.
			-Sprinkle with cheddar cheese.
			-Distribute parmesan over.
			-Bake 10 minutes in a 350 degree oven.

SAUTE DE POULET AUX CHAMPIGNONS

CHICKEN AND MUSHROOMS IN CREAM SAUCE

Sauteed chicken breasts are combined with carrots, celery, onions and mushrooms and garnished with a vinegarmustard cream sauce served on a bed of noodles.

1	tsp	Salt	-Blend salt, peppers, garlic powder and
1/4	tsp	Red pepper	thyme together.
1/4	tsp	Black pepper	-Add to melted butter.
1/8	tsp	Garlic powder	-Cut chicken breasts in half or thirds.
1/2	tsp	Thyme	-Coat with seasoned butter.
3	tbs	Butter, melted	-Saute chicken pieces in heated oil for 5 to 8
2	lbs	Chicken breast halves, deboned	minutes.
2	tbs	Peanut oil	-Remove to a serving platter and keep warm.
2	tbs	Butter	-Pour off the cooking oil.
1	sm	Onion, chopped	-Add the butter.
2	sm	Carrots, chopped	-Add the carrots, celery and onions.
2	ribs	Celery, chopped	-Saute for 3 to 4 minute.
1	lb	Mushrooms, sliced	-Add the mushrooms.
		Salt and pepper	-Salt and pepper and mix well.
1	tbs	Vinegar	-Cook for about 5 to 8 minutes.
1	tbs	Dijon mustard	-Remove from skillet and add to chicken.
1	cup	Cream	-Turn heat high and add vinegar and
		Parsley, chopped	mustard.
			-Add cream and reduce by one third.
			-Pour over chicken and mushrooms.
			-Garnish with parsley.
			-Serve with rice or noodles.

BALLOTTINE DE POULET

The whole deboned chicken is stuffed with a savory stuffing and baked. When sliced, it presents beautiful slices of chicken and the ingredients in the stuffing. Very elegant and not difficult to prepare.

1	4lb	Chicken	-Debone whole chicken.
1	clove	Garlic	-Crush garlic and spread over the chicken.
2	tbs	Butter	-Salt and pepper.
		Salt and pepper	-Set aside.

FARCI

1		Chicken liver, chopped	-Melt butter in skillet.
1 1/4	lbs	Mushrooms, chopped	-Saute onions and celery.
7	oz	Bacon, chopped	-Remove and set aside.
3 1/2	oz	Sausage meat	-Saute mushrooms quickly.
3 1/2	oz	Bread	-Add to onions and celery.
3 1/2	oz	Green olives stuffed	-Saute the bacon, liver and sausage about 5 minutes.
2	tbs	Parsley, chopped	-Pour the contents of the skilled into the vegetables.
1	tbs	Basil, fresh, chopped	
1		Onion, chopped	-Salt and pepper to taste.
4	stalks	Celery, chopped	-Add nutmeg.
1		Egg, beaten	-Mix well and let cool.
3/4	cup	Milk	-Add bread to milk and heat just to boiling.
1 3/4	oz	Butter	-Add to mixture.
		Salt and pepper	-Add eggs, parsley and basil mixing well.
		Nutmeg, ground	-Spread half the mixture over chicken.

-Spread olives over.
-Spread rest of mixture.
-Roll cnicken into the shape of a roast.
-Tie with kitchen string.
-Salt and pepper.
-Butter a baking dish.
-Place chicken on dish.
-Bake at 375 degrees for 1 hour 45 minutes.
-Allow to cool totally.

Three and one half pounds of cooked chicken will yield three cups chicken meat.

ESCALOPES DE DINDE AU FOUR

BAKED TURKEY SCALLOPS

Turkey parts are more and more available year around. The escalopes are obtained by cutting slices of the turkey breast horizontally with the grain rather than vertically through the flesh. An excellent substitute for veal.

6-8		Slices of turkey breast
2		Onions, chopped
4		Green onions, chopped
1	clove	Garlic, chopped
4	stems	Parsly, chopped
1/4	tsp	Thyme
4	tbs	Butter
1	cup	White wine
		Salt and pepper

-Melt one half the butter.
-Blend the butter, onions, green onions, garlic, parsley and thyme together.
-Salt and pepper the turkey slices.
-Pass them in the butter and seasoning mixture.
-Place the turkey in a baking dish.
-Pour the remaining butter mixture over.
-Add the wine.
-Place bits of the remaining butter over turkey.
-Bake at 350 degrees for 30 minutes.
-Turn turkey slices half way through cooking.
-Serve in baking dish.

DINDE AU FOUR

BAKED TURKEY

On our one hour Thanksgiving show, we prepared a traditional turkey with a Cajun flair. A sauteed mixture of aromatic vegetables with Cajun seasonings was worked between the skin and the flesh of the breast, thighs and legs. When roasted, the bird is extremely moist and has a wonderful flavor of Creole/Cajun character.

2	tbs	Butter
1	cup	Green onions, chopped
1/2	cup	Celery, chopped
1/2	cup	Bell pepper, chopped
3	cloves	Garlic, chopped
2	tbs	Lemon juice
1	tbs	Worchestershire
1/2	tsp	Thyme
1/4	tsp	Cayenne
1/4	tsp	Black pepper
1/2	tsp	Salt
1	12 lb	Turkey
		Poultry seasoning
2		Onions, whole
3	stalks	Celery
2	tbs	Butter

-Melt butter in a skillet.
-Add onions and saute 2 minutes.
-Add celery, bell pepper and garlic.
-Saute 5 minutes.
-Add lemon juice and worchestershire.
-Add thyme, cayenne, black pepper and salt.
-Cook until most of the liquid has evaporated.
-Cool.
-Gently separate the skin from the breast, thighs and legs of turkey.
-Spread seasoning mixture between skin and the flesh.
-Place one whole onion and a celery stalk in the cavity of the turkey.
-Place second onion in neck cavity.
-Close cavities with skewers.
-Rub outside of bird with butter.
-Sprinkle liberally with poultry seasoning.
-Place in a roasting pan.
-Cover loosely with aluminum foil.
-Roast at 325 degrees for four hours, (20 minutes per pound).
-Baste frequently.
-Remove from the oven.
-Let rest 15 minutes.
-Carve and serve.

PAIN DE MAIS FARCI

CORN BREAD DRESSING

Corn bread blended with lots of aromatic vegetables, seasonings and chicken stock can be used to stuff a turkey or hen or served as a casserole is truly a southern classic.

2	recipes	Corn bread
2	cups	French bread, cubed
2	tbs	Butter
2	cups	Onion, chopped
2	cups	Green onions, chopped
1 1/2	cups	Celery, chopped
2	cloves	Garlic, chopped
1/2	cup	Parsley, chopped
3		Eggs, beaten
1	tsp	Thyme
1	tbs	Poultry seasoning
		Salt and pepper
1	qt	Chicken stock

-Crumble corn bread into a large mixing bowl.
-Add bread cubes.
-Saute onions, green onions, celery and garlic in butter.
-Add to corn bread mixture.
-Add eggs, thyme, poultry seasoning, salt and pepper.
-Blend in enough stock to make a mixture which is moist but not too liquid.
-Pour into a casserole.
-Bake for 45 to 60 minutes at 325 degrees.

PAIN DE MAIS

CORN BREAD

3/4	cup	Cornmeal
1/3	cup	Flour
2	tsp	Baking powder
1	pinch	Salt
2		Eggs
1/3	cup	Milk

-Mix cornmeal, flour, salt, sugar, baking powder and eggs.
-Add milk and mix well.
-In a black iron skillet, heat a small amount (1 tablespoon) oil.
-When good and hot, pour into mixture (reserve a little in the skillet).
-Pour mixture into skillet and heat over medium heat for 1/2 minute.
-Place in 400 degree oven for about 15 minutes until brown.

SAUCE AUX GESIERS

GIBLET GRAVY

One of my Mother's best recipes handed down from the past, this giblet gravy was always served with holiday birds.

1	lb	Chicken gizzards
1	tbs	Butter
4	tbs	Flour
2		Onions
		Salt
		Pepper
1	can	Mushrooms
1/2	cup	Water

-Clean gizzards and chop into small pieces.
-Chop onions very fine.
-Make a dark roux.
-Add onions and saute.
-Add salt and pepper to taste.
-Add mushrooms and liquid.
-Add water.
-Add gizzards.
-Cook on slow heat for 1 hour or more until gizzards are tender.
-Add water if necessary.

Vegetables

VEGETABLES

FONDS D'ARTICHAUTS-SAUCE BEARNAISE
    ARTICHOKE BOTTOMS WITH BEARNAISE SAUCE

ARTICHAUTS AU GRATIN
    ARTICHOKES AU GRATIN

ASPERGES ROULEE AU JAMBON
    ASPARAGUS HAM ROLLS

CHOUX DE BRUXELLES ETUVEE AU BEURRE
    BRUSSELS SPROUTS BRAISED IN BUTTER

CHOU ROUGE AUX EPICES
    SPICED RED CABBAGE

CHOU CHINOIS AUX CHAMPIGNONS
    CHINESE CABBAGE WITH MUSHROOMS

CAROTTES HAALVA
    CARROTS HAALVA

CHOUFLEURS AU GRAITIN
    CAULIFLOWER CASSEROLE

CELERIS BRAISEE
    BRAISED CELERY

MAIS ESPAGNOLE
    SPANISH CORN

BEIGNETS DE MAIS
    CORN FRITTERS

RATATOUILLE NICOISE
    SMOTHERED EGGPLANT

FINOCCHI AL BURRO
    FENNEL SAUTEED IN BUTTER

FENOUIL A LA TOMATO
    FENNEL AND TOMATOES

PECHES EPICE
    SPICED PEACHES

POMMES AU POIVREES
    PEPPERED APPLES

HARICOTS VERTS LYONNAISE
    GREEN BEANS LYONNAISE

HARICOTS VERTS CREOLE
CREOLE GREEN BEANS

OIGNONS AU FOUR
ROASTED ONIONS

OIGNONS FARCIS
STUFFED ONIONS

OIGNONS ESCOFFIER
ONIONS ESCOFFIER

OIGNONS AU GRATIN
ONION CASSEROLE

GATEAU DE POMMES DE TERRE
POTATO CAKE

CREPES ALA POMMES DE TERRE
POTATO AND APPLE PANCAKES

POMMES DE TERRE ANNA
BAKED POTATO CAKE

POMMES DE TERRE MAGGIE ALLEN
BAKED SKILLET POTATOES

POMMES DE TERRE AU FOUR GALANTE
ELEGANT BAKED POTATOES

POMME DE TERRE DES NONNETTES
CONVENT-STYLE BAKED POTATOES

POMME DE TERRE DUCHESSE
DUCHESSE POTATOES

TOMATES FARCIS AVEC MAIS ET POIS
TOMATOES FILLED WITH CORN AND PEAS

TOMATES CREOLE
CREOLE TOMATES

COURGES JAUNE ET OIGNONS BRAISEE
BRAISED YELLOW SQUASH AND ONION

POTIRON D'ORANGE
PUMPKIN IN ORANGE SHELLS

COURGETTES NICOISE
ZUCCHINI NICOISE

CHARTREUSE AU LEGUMES
MOLD OF VEGETABLES

VEGETABLES

In Volume I we presented the vegetable recipes in order by their location on the plant from which they come; i.e., root, stem, leaf, flower, fruit, seeds and fungi.
This unfortunately caused some confusion - therefore we have listed them in strict alphabetic sequence.

FONDS D'ARTICHAUTS-SAUCE BEARNAISE
ARTICHOKE BOTTOMS WITH BEARNAISE SAUCE

TO COOK ARTICHOKE BOTTOMS: Wash artichokes and cut off stems even with the base. Cut off leaves 1/2 inch from the bottom. If there are any prickley tips left on, trim off. Rub lemon juice over the cut surface to prevent discoloration. Place in a saucepan, pouring boiling water to cover, and add 1 teaspoon salt and 1 teaspoon lemon juice. Cover and cook 30 to 40 minutes, or until the bottoms are tender. Drain well. Remove chokes from the centers. Fill with bearnaise sauce. Run under the broiler for 1 minute.

ARTICHAUTS AU GRATIN
ARTICHOKES AU GRATIN

Hearts of artichokes are blended with a bechamel sauce and covered with cheese for a casserole that will bring you praise.

2	9oz pks	Artichoke hearts
1	tbs	Lemon juice
1/4	cup	Butter
	Dash	White pepper
3/4	tsp	Salt
1	tsp	Onion salt
1/4	tsp	Dry mustard
1/3	cup	All purpose flour
1/2	cup	Reserved artichoke liquid
1 1/2	cup	Hot milk
1		Egg, slightly beaten
1/2	cup	Grated Swiss cheese
2	tbs	Bread crumbs
		Paprika

-Cook artichoke hearts according to package directions adding lemon juice to water.
-Drain, reserving 1/2 cup liquid.
-Place artichoke hearts in a single layer in a 9 inch shallow casserole.
-Melt butter in saucepan.
-Add pepper, salt, onion salt, mustard and flour; stir until smooth.
-Add gradually the artichoke liquid and milk; cook, stirring constantly until thickened.
-Remove from heat; add eggs and half of cheese.
-Stir until blended.
-Pour over artichokes.
-Sprinkle with remaining cheese, bread crumbs and paprika.
-Bake for 15 minutes at 450 degrees.

ASPERGES ROULEE AU JAMBON

ASPARAGUS HAM ROLLS

On our Fourth of July one hour special show, asparagus rolled in ham slices was one of many dishes for our all cold meal.

15-20		Fresh asparagus
1/2	cup	Mayonnaise
1	tbs	Dijon mustard
15-20	slices	Boiled ham
3	tbs	Lemon juice
		Salt and pepper
2	tbs	Olive oil

-Break off stems of asparagus.
-Peel asparagus with vegetable peeler.
-Place in cold salted water and bring to a boil.
-Simmer about 5 minutes.
-Drain and refresh in cold water.
-Chill.
-Blend mayonnaise and mustard.
-Spread thin layer of mustard mayonnaise on a slice of boiled ham.
-Place an asparagus on ham so that about 1 inch of asparagus is over the edge of ham.
-Roll ham around asparagus.
-Arrange on a serving dish.
-Blend lemon juice, salt and pepper.
-Wisk in olive oil.
-Pour over ham/asparagus rolls.

CAROTTES HAALVA

CARROTS HAALVA

Another of cooking teacher Joe Middleton's unique recipes he brought to Pensacola. Carrots, after a long cooking in milk, are blended with raisins, almonds and brown sugar. Delicious.

1 1/2	lb	Carrots, peeled and grated
3	cups	Milk
1/2	cup	Clarified butter
1/4	cup	Raisins
1/4	cup	Slivered almonds (toasted)
3-4	tbs	Brown sugar
1	tsp	Cardamon (optional)

-In a saucepan, combine grated carrots and milk.
-Heat and simmer for 1 to 1 1/2 hours until milk has evaporated (drain).
-In a skillet heat clarified butter.
-Add brown sugar and cardamon.
-Stir.
-Add cooled (drained) carrots.
-Saute until mixture is evenly blended.
-Add raisins and almonds.

CHOUX DE BRUXELLES ETUVEE AU BEURRE

BRUSSELS SPROUTS BRAISED IN BUTTER

Onions, bay leaf and cloves give these bright green brussels sprouts a distinct flavor. After braising they are sauteed in a little buttter to enchance the taste.

1	qt	Brussels sprouts	-Place brussels sprouts in water to cover.
1	sm	Onion, sliced	-Bring to a boil.
1		Bay leaf	-Add onions, bay leaf, cloves and salt.
2		Cloves	-Simmer 12 to 15 minutes.
1	tsp	Salt	-Drain.
4	tbs	Butter	-Melt butter in a large skillet.
		Salt	-Add brussels sprouts.
		White pepper	-Saute over low heat for 5 minutes.
2	tbs	Chives	-Salt and pepper to taste.
			-Sprinkle with chives.
			-Place in a serving dish.

CELERIS BRAISEE

BRAISED CELERY

Celery, most often eaten raw, is a wonderful vegetable when cooked. Here it is braised with carrots and onions in chicken stock.

1/2	lb	Celery hearts	-Cut celery branches into about 4 inch lengths.
1	lg	Onion, chopped	-Saute onions and carrots in the butter for 5 minutes.
2	sm	Carrots, chopped	
1	tbs	Butter	-Add the celery and toss about 2 minutes.
6	cups	Chicken stock	-Remove from the fire.
1	tbs	Parsley, chopped	-Place contents of skillet in a baking dish.
		Salt and pepper	-Salt and pepper lightly.
			-Add the chicken stock.
			-Cover and bake at 350 degrees for 1 hour.
			-At serving, sprinkle with parsley.

CHOU CHINOIS AUX CHAMPIGNONS

CHINESE CABBAGE WITH MUSHROOMS

Elongated, loose leaf Chinese cabbage is stir-fried with mushrooms in a light sauce of soy, sherry and stock. Quick, easy and delicious.

1	lb	Cabbage
1/2	lb	Mushrooms
3	tbs	Peanut oil
2	tbs	Cornstarch
1	tbs	Soy sauce
1	tbs	Sherry
1	cup	Chicken stock
1/2	tsp	Sesame oil (optional)

-Separate the cabbage leaves and cut into pieces.
-Cut the mushrooms into halves or quarters.
-Heat the oil in a wok or deep skillet.
-Add the mushrooms and the cabbage.
-Turn well and cook about 3 minutes.
-Blend the cornstarch with the soy sauce and sherry.
-Add the chicken stock and soy/cornstarch mixture.
-Toss well until sauce thickens.
-Remove from heat.
-Add the sesame oil (optional).

One half pound of fresh mushrooms will yield about two and one half cups sliced.

CHOU ROUGE AUX EPICES

SPICED RED CABBAGE

Flavorful red cabbage is braised with herbes and spices then enriched with cream.

1 1/2	lbs	Red cabbage
2	cups	Water
2	tsp	Caraway seed
1/2	tsp	Quatre-espices*
2	tbs	Wine vinegar
3	tbs	Cream

-Shred cabbage.
-Bring water to a boil in a saute pan.
-Add the cabbage, vinegar, caraway and Quatre-espices.
-Cover and cook 10 to 12 minutes turning from time to time.
-Place cabbage on a serving plate.
-Add cream and toss.

One lb cabbage, shredded yields 4 cups raw and 3 cups cooked.

CHOUFLEURS AU GRAITIN

CAULIFLOWER CASSEROLE

This was one of my mother's Thanksgiving tratitions. Blanched cauliflower is covered with a mushroom bechamel sauce and mixed with American or chedder cheese for a distinct casserole.

1	lg	Cauliflower, cleaned and separated
1/2	lb	American cheese
1/2	lb	Mushrooms, sliced
1	recipe	Bechamel sauce

-Blanch cauliflower in salted water for 10 minutes.
-Drain.
-Arrange in a baking dish.
-Add 3/4 of the cheese in and around cauliflower.
-Saute mushrooms in butter until butter is absorbed.
-Add to bechamel sauce.
-Pour over cauliflower/cheese mixture.
-Sprinkle remaining cheese on top.
-Bake at 325 degrees for 45 minutes until cheese has browned.
-Reheat at serving time.

To BLANCH is the cooking process whereby food, usually vegetables, are plunged into rapidly boiling water, the water returned to the boil and the food cooked for a few minutes. The food is usually drained and REFRESHED in cold water.

BEIGNETS DE MAIS

CORN FRITTERS

Baking powder and beaten egg whites cause this corn batter to inflate when fried in hot oil. They are light and fluffy and so good.

2		Eggs
1/2	cup	Whole kernal corn
1/2	cup	Creamed corn
1/8	tsp	Salt
1	oz	Milk
1/2	cup	Flour
1	tsp	Baking powder

-Separate eggs.
-Add yolks to corn.
-Beat egg whites.
-Add salt.
-Add milk to corn.
-Add flour and baking powder.
-Fold in egg whites.
-Drop by tablespoonsful in hot (325 degree) oil.
-Fry until golden.

MAIS ESPAGNOLE

SPANISH CORN

Kernels of corn are cooked in a tomato sauce and seasoned with bacon for a very flavorful dish.

1	doz	Ears corn	
1	lg	Can tomato sauce	
3	lg	Onions, chopped	
1	lb	Bacon	
1 1/2	tsp	Baking soda	
		Salt and pepper	

-Remove corn kernels from cobs.
-Fry bacon crisp - save.
-Add corn and tomato sauce to bacon
    drippings and cook slowly 45 to 60 minutes
    (stir frequently, it burns easily).
-Add additional bacon drippings if necessary.
-Add salt and pepper and baking soda.
-Remove from heat.
-Crumble bacon over top before serving.

RATATOUILLE NICOISE

SMOTHERED EGGPLANT

Zucchini, eggplant, tomatoes, green peppers and onions are braised in olive oil and their natural juices and spiced with garlic and parsley to create a classic dish from Nice, France.

2		Zucchini	
1		Eggplant	
4		Tomatoes	
2		Sweet peppers	
1/2	cup	Sliced onions	
1/4	cup	Olive oil	
1	clove	Garlic	
1/2	tsp	Sugar	
		Pepper	
		Salt	
		Parsley	

-Cut zucchini and eggplant into slices 1/8
    inch thick.
-Peel and dice tomatoes.
-Slice sweet pepper.
-Saute onions in oil.
-Add tomatoes - cook 1 minute.
-Add zucchini, eggplant, peppers, garlic,
    sugar, salt and pepper.
-Cover.
-Bring to a boil.
-Cook 2 minutes.
-Remove cover.
-Cook until liquid has evaporated.
-Sprinkle with parsley.
-Serve.

FINOCCHI AL BURRO

FENNEL SAUTEED IN BUTTER

This anise flavored celery type vegetable is delicious when simply boiled, sauced with butter flavored with spices and garnished with parmesan.

4		Fennel bulbs
6	tbs	Butter
1/2	tbs	Olive oil
		Salt
		Pepper
		Nutmeg, grated
1/4	cup	Parmesan cheese

-Cut fennel bulbs into quarters vertically (eights if large).
-Add to boiling salted water.
-Cook about 15 to 20 minutes until cooked but still firm.
-Drain and dry.
-Heat butter and oil in skillet.
-Add fennel.
-Sprinkle with salt, pepper and nutmeg.
-Saute 5 minutes.
-Sprinkle with parmesan.
-Toss for a few minutes.
-Transfer to a serving plate.

FENOUIL A LA TOMATO

FENNEL AND TOMATOES

The mild liquorish taste of fennel combines with the tomatoes producing a fragrant and colorful vegetable.

2	lbs	Fennel
1/2	lb	Tomatoes, peeled
1	lg	Onion, chopped
1	clove	Garlic, chopped
2	tbs	Butter
		Salt and pepper

-Cut fennel bulbs into slices.
-Boil for 10 minutes in salted water, then drain.
-Cut the tomatoes into quarters.
-Saute onions and garlic in butter for 5 minutes.
-Add the fennel.
-Toss and cook one minute.
-Salt and pepper the vegetables.
-Add the tomatoes and cook on medium heat for 15 minutes.
-Place the fennel and the juices on a serving platter.

PECHES EPICE

SPICED PEACHES

Peaches are poached in a liquid of simple syrup and vinegar spiced with cinnamon, cloves and peppercorns. They were a garnish around the crown roast of pork on the special one hour Christmas show.

4	cups	Peach halves and the juice from the can
		Wine vinegar
		Whole cloves
1		Cinnamon stick
1	tsp	Peppercorns
1/2	tsp	Mace
1/2	tsp	Allspice

-Drain syrup from cans of peaches and reserve.
-Insert two cloves into each peach.
-Add half again as much wine vinegar to the peach syrup.
-Add cinnamon stick, mace and allspice.
-Bring syrup to a boil.
-Reduce to a simmer.
-Place peaches in sauce.
-Gently poach for 5 minutes.
-Turn heat off.
-Let peaches marinate in syrup for one or two hours.
-Reheat at serving time.

POMMES AU POIVREES

PEPPERED APPLES

Three kinds of pepper are combined with green onions and butter to saute apples for an excellent accompaniment to pork or chicken dishes. Unusual and delicious.

6		Apples, peeled and cored
4	oz	Butter, clarified
6		Green onions, chopped
1/8	tsp	White pepper
1/8	tsp	Black pepper
1/8	tsp	Cayenne pepper
1/2	tsp	Salt

-Cut each apple into 8 slices.
-Saute apple slices in butter for two minutes.
-Add green onions..
-Mix well.
-Lower heat to simmer.
-Cook for 5 minutes.
-Add peppers and salt.
-Cook 2 or 3 minutes or until apples are tender.

HARICOTS VERTS LYONNAISE

GREEN BEANS LYONNAISE

Blanched and refreshed green beans are sauteed with onions and flavored with a little vinegar. Delicious!

1	lb	Beans
2 1/2	tbs	Butter
2	med	Onions, sliced thin
		Salt and black pepper
1	tbs	Finely chopped parsley or chervil
1	tbs	Wine vinegar

-Place beans in a large pot of boiling salted water and boil, uncovered, about 8 minutes.
-Saute onions in butter over medium heat.
-Refresh green beans in cold water. Drain and dry.
-Place beans in the pan wih onions and raise heat to med-high.
-Shake the pan to toss them about until they are lightly browned.
-Season to taste with salt and pepper.
-Sprinkle with the vinegar.
-Remove from heat, sprinkle with parsley and serve.

To REFRESH means to drench hot foods which have been BLANCHED in cold water until the food is room temperature. This stops the cooking and sets the color. Foods which have been blanched can be reheated in a small amount of butter or flavored stock in a skillet at serving time.

HARICOTS VERTS CREOLE

CREOLE GREEN BEANS

Green beans combine wih chili sauce, onions, ham and bacon for a Creole taste.

2	lbs	Green beans
1/4	lb	Bacon cut in 1/2 inch pieces
1/2	cup	Green onions, sliced
1	clove	Garlic, chopped
1/2	cup	Chili sauce
1/4	lb	Boiled ham, diced

-Cook beans in boiling salted water until tender.
-Refresh in cold water.
-Drain well.
-Cook bacon in a large skillet.
-Remove bacon and reserve.
-Discard all but 1 tablespoon fat.
-Add onions and saute.
-Add garlic and chili sauce.
-Bring to a boil.
-Simmer 5 minutes.
-Stir in green beans, ham and bacon.
-Simmer 5 minutes.

OIGNONS AU FOUR

Simple and flavorful, onions are baked in their skins then peeled and garnished with butter and paprika.

6		Spanish onions
6	tbs	Butter
		Salt
		Paprika
		Parsley, chopped

-Line a roasting pan with foil.
-Cut root from unpeeled onions.
-Place in roasting pan.
-Bake at 350 degrees for 2 hours.
-Remove from oven.
-Peel off the skins.
-Place onions on a serving dish.
-Spread tops slightly with a pointed knife.
-Insert a piece of butter into.
-Sprinkle with salt, paprika and parsley.

OIGNONS FARCIS

Onions hollowed out to form a cup or container are stuffed with a sausage force meat and braised in chicken stock. Onion lovers beware!

8	lg	White onions
1/4	cup	Butter
1/2	lb	Sausage meat
1 1/4	cups	Bread crumbs
1/3	cup	Light cream
1/4	cup	Chopped parsley
1/4	tsp	Thyme
		Salt and pepper
1	cup	Beef stock
1/2	cup	White wine

-Scoop out centers of onions leaving a shell about 1/4 inch thick.
-Chop onion centers to make 1 1/2 cups.
-Blanch onion cases for 5 minutes.
-Turn upside down to drain.
-Saute onions in butter.
-Add sausage meat and saute.
-Soak bread crumbs in cream then drain.
-Add bread crumbs, parsley, thyme, salt and pepper.
-Season onion shells with salt and pepper.
-Fill with sausage mixture.
-Arrange in a buttered baking dish.
-Pour 1 cup beef stock and the wine around onions.
-Dot with butter and bring liquid to a boil.
-Bake in 350 degree oven basting for about 45 minutes.
-Transfer onions to serving dish.
-Reduce juices by half.
-Pour over onions.
-Sprinkle with chopped parsley.

OIGNONS ESCOFFIER

ONIONS ESCOFFIER

The famous French Chef Escoffier created many recipes which have remained classics. This one has filtered down to my files and may not be authentic, however, they are good.

40	sm	Boiling onions, peeled
2/3	cup	Olive oil
1/2	cup	Vinegar
1/2	cup	Madeira
2		Bay leaves
1	tsp	Thyme
1	tsp	Basil
1	tbs	Salt
1	tsp	Pepper
1	pinch	Saffron
2	tbs	Tomato paste
3/4	cup	Dark raisins

-Put onions in a deep skillet with oil, vinegar, wine, bay leaves, thyme, basil, salt, pepper and enough water to barely cover.
-Bring to a simmer for 15 minutes.
-Add saffron and tomato paste.
-Cook until tender.
-Add raisins.
-Cook 10 minutes.

To SIMMER, another form of boiling, is a method of cooking foods in liquids at a temperature of about 190 degrees, where the liquid displays small bubbles without the ingredients moving rapidly in the pot.

OIGNONS AU GRATIN

ONION CASSEROLE

Boiled onions are combined with a bechamel sauce and dill weed in a casserole dish and garnished with cheese.

12		White onions, peeled
8	tbs	Butter
1/2	cup	Flour
1	pt	Milk, heated
1	tsp	Dill weed
		Salt and pepper
1/2	cup	Cheddar cheese, grated

-Cook onions in boiling salted water about 20 minutes until tender.
-Melt butter in a saucepan.
-Add flour and cook about 1 or 2 minutes.
-Add the milk gradually while wisking.
-Add the dill weed, salt and pepper.
-Place onions in a casserole.
-Cover with the sauce.
-Sprinkle with cheese.
-Bake at 350 degrees until brown, about 20 30 minutes.

GATEAU DE POMMES DE TERRE

POTATO CAKE

Bacon, cheddar cheese and sliced potatoes are cooked slowly in bacon drippings. When unmolded, they form a potato cake which is garnished with parsley.

1/4	cup	Bacon, diced	-Heat bacon in heavy skillet until fat runs.
1/2	lb	Potatoes, thin sliced	(Moderate heat).
1/4	lb	Cheddar cheese, coarsely grated	-Add potatoes.
		Salt and pepper	-Cook 5 to 6 minutes stirring.
		Parsley, chopped	-Stir in the cheese.
			-Season with salt and pepper
			-Cook over gentle heat for 15 minutes.
			-Invert onto serving dish.
			-Garnish with parsley.

CREPES A LA POMMES DE TERRE

POTATO AND APPLE PANCAKES

Potatoes, apples and onions are blended with milk, eggs and flour to form a batter which is then sauteed like pancakes.

3		Potatoes, peeled	-Shred potatoes, apple and onion.
1		Apple, peeled	-Set aside.
1/2	sm	Onion, peeled	-Mix eggs, flour, milk, butter, salt and pepper.
2		Eggs	-Add to potatoes.
2	tbs	Flour	-Blend well.
2	tbs	Milk	-Drop 1/4 cup potato mixture onto hot
2	tbs	Butter, melted	greased skillet.
1/2	tsp	Salt	-Brown on one side.
		Pepper	-Turn.
			-Brown on the other side.

POMMES DE TERRE ANNA

BAKED POTATO CAKE

A French classic, sliced potatoes are baked in butter and reversed to form a cake. Delicious and beautiful to behold.

1/2	lb	Butter
3	lbs	Potatoes

-Preheat oven to 450 degrees.
-Clarify butter.
-Peel potatoes and cut into 1/8 inch rounds.
-Pour 1/4 inch butter into a heavy skillet and
set over moderate heat.
-Quickly arrange a layer of potatoes starting in
the center, overlapping until the pan is
covered.
-Pour a spoonful of butter over potatoes.
-Reversing directions, arrange another layer
of potatoes and sprinkle with more butter.
-Repeat until the pan is full.
-Press down hard with the bottom of a
buttered pan.
-Cover and bake in the middle rack for 30
minutes with a pan on the lower rack to catch
any drippings.
-Remove cover and bake 25 minutes more.
-Pour off excess butter and unmold on a
serving dish.
-Add salt and pepper at this time.

POMMES DE TERRE MAGGIE ALLEN

BAKED SKILLET POTATOES

Grated potatoes and eggs are baked in a black iron skillet in the manner of an Italian fritata. It is reversed onto a serving plate and cut into wedges with a spoonful of sour cream.

3	lbs	Potatoes, peeled and grated
8		Eggs
		Salt
		White pepper
2	tbs	Peanut oil
1	cup	Sour cream

-Rinse potatoes in cold water and drain.
-Squeeze in a towel to remove excess
moisture.
-Beat eggs, salt and pepper in a bowl.
-Add potatoes and mix well.
-Grease a black iron skillet with the oil.
-Preheat skillet in a 450 degree oven for 5
minutes.
-Fill casserole with potato mix.
-Cover and bake 1 hour.
-Serve with sour cream.

POMMES DE TERRE AU FOUR GALANTE

ELEGANT BAKED POTATOES

After peeling, these potatoes are sliced very thin almost all the way through and bathed in butter and paprika. They are then baked until brown and crispy - truly elegant.

1		Potato per person
1 1/2	tbs	Butter per potato, melted
		Paprika
		Salt
		White pepper

-Peel potatoes.
-Slice a thin layer off a longside.
-Slice potatoes 1/8 inch thick but not all the way through.
-Mix butter and paprika.
-Roll potatoes in butter/paprika mixture.
-Sprinkle with salt and pepper.
-Bake in a covered casserole for 30 minutes.
-Uncover and bake 45 minutes more until brown and crisp.

POMME DE TERRE DES NONNETTES

CONVENT-STYLE BAKED POTATOES

Small new potatoes are coated with egg, cheese and bread crumbs and baked with a little butter, which have taken the name of Convent Style.

2		Eggs
		Salt and pepper
12	sm	Round new potatoes
3/4	cup	Grated gruyere cheese
1	cup	Bread crumbs
2	tbs	Butter

-Peel potatoes.
-Beat eggs lightly with salt and pepper.
-Coat potatoes with egg mixture.
-Roll each in grated cheese.
-Roll in bread crumbs, pressing gently to make crumbs stick.
-Melt butter in shallow baking dish.
-Arrange potatoes in dish without touching.
-Bake 45 minutes at 450 degrees.

Root vegetables should start cooking in cold water. This allows the vegetable to heat uniformly as the water warms.

POMME DE TERRE DUCHESSE

DUCHESSE POTATOES

Mashed potatoes enriched with butter but no liquid are piped to form cups for vegetable fillings.

1 1/2	lbs	Potatoes, peeled
1/4	cup	Butter
2		Egg yolks
1	dash	Nutmeg
		Salt
		White pepper

-Boil potatoes about 20 minutes until done.
-Put potatoes through a ricer.
-Blend in butter.
-Add egg yolks, nutmeg, salt and pepper.
-Using a pastry bag with a star pipe potatoes into three inch circles on a greased cookie sheet.
-Pipe an additional ring around the edge of each circle to form a cup.
-Sprinkle with parmesan cheese.
-Bake at 350 for about 8 to 10 minutes until edges brown.
-Place on a serving dish and fill centers with a cooked vegetable of your choice.
   Suggestions: green peas, sliced carrots, sauteed mushrooms.

TOMATES FARCIS AVEC MAIS ET POIS

TOMATOES FILLED WITH CORN AND PEAS

This cold vegetable dish combines colorful yellow corn and green peas as a filling for scooped out tomato shells and garnished with a cream vinaigrette dressing. It was one of the vegetables we used for our Fourth of July one hour special all cold meal.

8		Tomatoes
1 1/2	cups	Corn, blanched
1 1/2	cups	Green peas, blanched
4	oz	Pimiento, chopped
1/3	cup	Parsley
1/2	cup	Green onions, chopped
1	tbs	Dijon mustard
4	tbs	Vinegar
2	tbs	Lemon juice
1/2	cup	Cream
		Salt and pepper

-Cut tops off tomatoes.
-Scoop out pulp.
-Mix well together the corn, peas, pimiento, parsley and onions.
-Fill tomato shells with vegetable mixture.
-Blend together the mustard, vinegar, lemon juice, salt and pepper.
-Pour in cream while blending.
-Pour about 2 tablespoons of cream dressing over corn and peas.
-Refrigerate until serving time.

TOMATES CREOLE

CREOLE TOMATOES

Tomatoes are layered with seasoned bread crumbs and butter in a casserole and baked to form a delicious creole dish.

6	lg	Tomatoes	-Scald and peel tomatoes.
		Seasoned bread crumbs	-Slice about 1/4 inch thick.
		Butter	-Place a layer of tomatoes in a baking dish.
		Salt and pepper	-Sprinkle generously with bread crumbs.
			-Salt and pepper.
			-Dot with butter.
			-Repeat layers of tomatoes, bread crumbs, salt, pepper and butter.
			-Bake at 350 degrees for 50 minutes.
			-Sprinkle with salt, pepper and nutmeg.

COURGES JAUNE ET OIGNONS BRAISEE

BRAISED YELLOW SQUASH AND ONION

Quick and easy, tasty yellow summer squash and onions are braised in chicken stock flavored with thyme providing a bright color and taste to any meal.

2	lbs	Yellow squash	-Cut squash into rounds.
1	lg	Onion	-Cut onions into rings.
3	tbs	Butter	-Mix together.
		Salt and pepper	-Melt butter in a skillet.
1/3	cup	Chicken stock	-Toss vegetables in butter.
1/4	tsp	Thyme	-Add salt, pepper and thyme.
			-Add chicken broth.
			-Cover.
			-Reduce heat to simmer.
			-Cook 15 to 20 minutes.
			-Remove cover.
			-Cook until liquid is almost gone.

POTIRON D'ORANGE

PUMPKIN IN ORANGE SHELLS

A great accompaniment for a baked turkey or pork roast are these orange shells filled with pureed pumpkin spiced with cinnamon and cloves.

6		Oranges	-Cut oranges in half.
2		Eggs, beaten	-Remove segments and reserve.
1	lb	Canned pumpkin	-Scoop out pulp and discard.
1/2	cup	Sugar	-Mix eggs, pumpkin, sugar, salt, cinnamon,
1/2	tsp	Salt	ginger, cloves and orange segments.
1	tsp	Cinnamon	-Fill orange shells with mixture.
1/2	tsp	Ginger	-Place in a casserole with 1/2 inch water.
1/4	tsp	Cloves	-Bake at 350 for 30 minutes.
1	cup	Orange segments	

COURGETTES NICOISE

ZUCCHINI NICOISE

Blanched and refreshed zucchini is sauced with an anchovy flavored vinaigrette. Can be served as a salad or as a cold vegetable at a summer meal.

4	med	Zucchini	-Cut zucchini into thick rounds.
1	lg	Lemon	-Blanch in boiling water about 5 to 7 minutes.
12		Anchovy filets	-Refresh in cold water.
3/4	cup	Olive oil	-Squeeze lemon into a bowl.
6		Black olives, pitted	-Crush 6 anchovy filets into the lemon juice.
1	clove	Garlic, crushed	-Add pepper to taste.
1/3	cup	Parsley, chopped	-Wisk in the olive oil.
		Pepper	-Arrange the zucchini on a serving platter.
			-Garnish with the remaining anchovy filets and the black olives.
			-Pour the dressing over all.
			-Sprinkle with the parsley.

CHARTREUSE AU LEGUMES

MOLD OF VEGETABLES

This beautiful display of molded vegetables will steal the show and bring raves from your guests. It is as delicious as it is beautiful. This presentation was prepared by Panama City, Florida, cooking school teacher, John Sherman.

1	lb	Green beans, cooked and cut to same size to fit mold vertically
2	lg	Yellow squash, cut in thin rounds and blanched
2	med	Zucchini, cut in thin rounds and blanched
2	med	Carrots, cut in wide julienne
1/4	cup	Green peas, frozen
1	cup	Brussels sprouts, blanched
1	cup	Cauliflower, blanched
6		Cabbage leaves, blanched
		Butter, softened
1 1/2	cup	Potatoes, mashed
1/4	cup	Butter, melted
		Salt and pepper

-All vegetables should be seasoned individually as they are cooked.
-Coat a 6 inch diameter mold generously with the softened butter.
-Place a row of green peas around the outside bottom edge of the mold.
-Place a row of overlapping slices of yellow squash on bottom of mold.
-Place a row of overlapping zucchini slices next to the squash to form an inner circle.
-Repeat squash and zucchini until bottom is covered.
-Alternate a green bean and a carrot strip standing upright against the side of the mold.
-Cover sides and bottom with a layer of mashed potatoes.
-Cover potatoes with cabbage leaves.
-Place an outer circle of brussels sprouts over cabbage.
-Make an inner circle with cauliflower.
-Repeat circles of squash, zucchini, sprouts and cauliflower until mold is full.
-Pour melted butter over vegetables.
-Cover with cabbage leaves.
-Add a final layer of potatoes.
-Bake at 350 degrees for 20 minutes.
-Remove from oven.
-Place a serving dish on top of mold.
-Reverse plate and mold.
-Remove plate.
-Garnish with half slices of cherry tomatoes around molded vegetables.

Rice and Pasta

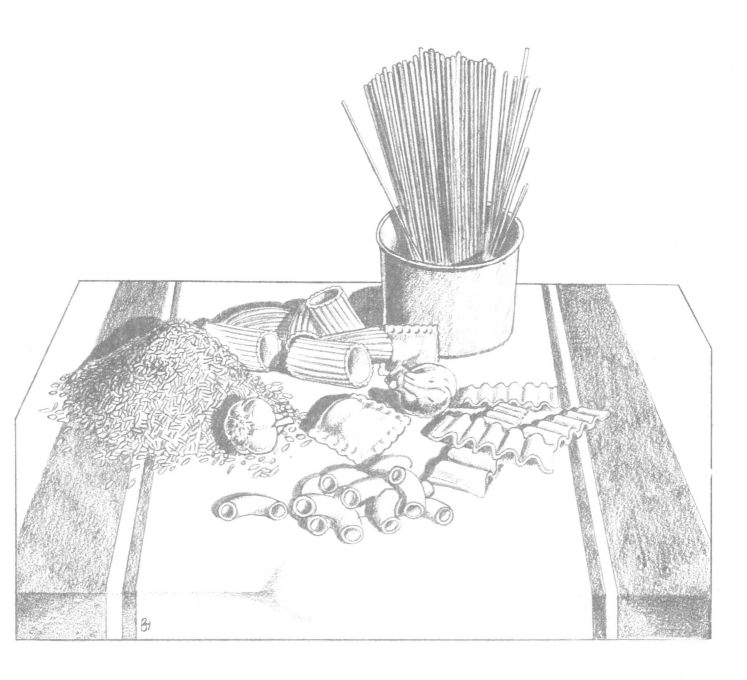

RICE AND PASTA

RIZ ET PETIT POIS
    RICE AND PEAS

RIZ AMANDINE AVEC CHAMPIGNONS
    ALMOND RICE WITH MUSHROOMS

RIZ AU CITRON
    LEMON RICE WITH GREEN PEAS

FARCIS AU RIZ
    RICE DRESSING

NOUILLES A L'ALLEMAGNE
    GERMAN NOODLES

NOUILLES VERTS A LA MAISON
    GREEN NOODLES WITH PEAS

NOUILLES ET PETIT POIS
    BUTTERED NOODLES AND GREEN PEAS

LA SPADELLATA
    SPAGHETTI IN CREAM-TOMATO SAUCE

FETTUCCINE AU FOUR
    BAKED FETTUCCINE

SOUFFLE DE NOUILLES
    PASTA SOUFFLE

GNOCCHI A LA ROMANO
    GNOCCHI ROMAN STYLE

SPAGHETTI CARUSO
    SPAGHETTI WITH CHICKEN LIVERS

LASAGNA FRUITS DE MER
    MIXED SEAFOOD LASAGNA

PASTA A LA TERESA TURCI
    PASTA WITH MEATBALLS, CHICKEN, AND MUSHROOMS

NOUILLES SAUTEES CHOW MEIN
    CHOW MEIN

NOUILLES CHINOISE FRITES
    FRIED CHINESE NOODLES (CHOW MEIN)

RICE AND PASTA

Rice, the staple of Creole cuisine, and pasta, the Italian base are presented here in some interesting recipes. My favorites are the Almond Rice with Mushrooms and the Spaghetti Caruso. I hope you enjoy them all.

RIZ ET PETIT POIS

RICE AND PEAS

Lettuce and green peas give a special taste to rice cooked in chicken broth with butter and parmesan for the final garnish.

1/2		Onion, chopped
1/2	cup	Lettuce, chopped
		Olive oil
1/2	cup	Chicken broth
3	cups	Peas
1/2	cup	Water
2	cups	Half cooked rice
2	cups	Broth
2	tbs	Butter
1	cup	Parmesan cheese
		Salt

-Saute onions and lettuce in olive oil until onions are yellow.
-Add broth.
-In another pan saute peas in butter for 3 minutes.
-Add rice and broth.
-Reduce heat.
-Simmer 10-15 minutes.
-Add butter and cheese.
-Salt to taste.

RIZ AMANDINE AVEC CHAMPIGNONS

ALMOND RICE WITH MUSHROOMS

The nutty flavor of brown rice blends with toasted almonds and mushrooms to form a molded rice dish. Good with ham dishes.

1/2	cup	Almonds, sliced and toasted
3	tbs	Butter
1/2	lb	Mushrooms, sliced
4	cups	Brown rice, cooked
		Salt and pepper
		Cherry tomatoes

-In a large skillet saute mushrooms.
-Add almonds and rice.
-Salt and pepper to taste.
-Place mixture in a buttered mold.
-Place in a 350 oven for 5 minutes.
-Unmold on a serving platter.
-Garnish with cherry tomatoes.

One cup white long grain rice absorbs 2 cups liquid.

RIZ AU CITRON

LEMON RICE WITH GREEN PEAS

Rice is boiled in stock and vermouth with turmeric then garnished with lemon zest and parsley. It is a good accompaniment to fish dishes.

2	tbs	Butter	-Melt butter in a saucepan.
1 1/4	cups	Rice	-Add rice and saute 1 minute.
1/4	cup	Dry vermouth	-Add broth, vermouth, salt, pepper and
2 1/4	cups	Chicken stock	turmeric.
1	tsp	Turmeric	-Bring to a boil.
3/4	tsp	Salt	-Reduce to a simmer and cover.
		Pepper	-Cook 18 to 20 minutes.
		Zest of 1 lemon	-Add lemon zest and parsley.
2	tbs	Parsley, chopped	-Place in a buttered mold.
1	pkg	Frozen green peas, cooked	-Place in a 350 degree oven for 5 minutes.
			-Unmold on a serving plate.
			-Surround with green peas.

One cup white long grain rice yields 3 cups cooked.

FARCIS AU RIZ

RICE DRESSING

This very old rice dressing is excellent for stuffing a turkey or simply cooked in a casserole.

2	cups	Brown rice (or wild rice)	-Fry chicken livers, chop and set aside.
2	med	Onions	-Boil rice as directed and steam.
8-10		Chicken livers	-Saute onions in oil.
1	cup	Chopped walnuts	-Add chopped chicken livers.
1/2	cup	Finely chopped celery	-Add chopped walnuts.
1	lb	Mushroom, sliced	-Add celery.
		Salt	-Cook above ingredients 2-3 minutes on
1/4	tsp	Sage	moderate heat.
1/4	tsp	Oregano	-Add mushrooms and remove from heat.
		Pepper	-Add herbs and seasoning.
		Celery seed	-Mix all above well.
10		Anise seeds	-Add sherry.
		Sherry	-Mix above with rice.
			-Place in casserole.
			-Cover and bake 1/2 hour - add 1/4 cup
			water if too dry.
			-Good for stuffing for fowl, eggplant, bell
			pepper or other meats.

One cup brown rice (unpolished) yields 2 ½ cups cooked.

Eight ounces (½ lb) spaghetti yields 4 cups cooked.

NOUILLES A L'ALLEMAGNE

GERMAN NOODLES

Sauteed mushrooms and boiled noodles are layered in a casserole and sprinkled with bread crumbs. It is then run in the oven to brown the top producing a dish that will surprise you.

1	lb	Mushrooms, sliced	-Preheat oven to 375 degrees.
2	tbs	Butter	-Saute mushrooms in butter 5 minutes.
		Salt	-Season with salt, pepper and parsley.
		Pepper	-Arrange noodles and mushrooms in layers in
		Parsley, chopped	a greased 6 cup casserole.
8	oz	Noodles, cooked	-Top with buttered bread crumbs.
2	tbs	Bread crumbs	-Brown in the oven about 10 minutes.

NOUILLES VERTS A LA MAISON

GREEN NOODLES WITH PEAS

Green spinach noodles combine well with green peas and butter for an interesting taste and color combination.

8	oz	Spinach noodles	-Boil noodles in boiling water until al dente.
3	qts	Boiling water	-Drain and return to pot.
1	tsp	Salt	-Add green peas and butter.
2	cups	Green peas, cooked	-Toss well.
4	oz	Butter	-Salt and pepper to taste.
		Cracked pepper	
		Salt	

One cup uncooked noodles produces 1 3/4 cups cooked.

NOUILLES ET PETIT POIS

BUTTERED NOODLES AND GREEN PEAS

Rosemary imparts its special flavor to noodles and peas cooked together.

4	qts	Boiling water
2	tsp	Salt
1	lb	Egg noodles
1	pkg	Frozen green peas
4	tbs	Butter
		Salt and pepper
1/2	tsp	Rosemary

-Into boiling salted water place egg noodles and green peas.
-Cook until pasta is al dente.
-Drain.
-Place butter in same pot used for boiling.
-Return noodles and peas to pot.
-Sprinkle with rosemary.
-Toss well.
-Turn into a serving dish.

To help prevent pasta from sticking together when boiling place about 1 tablespoon of cooking oil or margarine in the water.

LA SPADELLATA

SPAGHETTI IN CREAM-TOMATO SAUCE

Pasta dressed with a light cream tomato sauce and garnished with parmesan is a delicious dish.

5	qts	Water
1 1/2	tsp	Salt
1	lb	Spaghetti
1	pt	Light cream
1 1/2	tbs	Tomato paste
1/3	cup	Parmesan cheese

-Bring water to a boil.
-Add salt and spaghetti.
-Return to a boil.
-Pour cream into a skillet over low heat (do not boil).
-Add tomato paste.
-Drain spaghetti.
-Place in a serving dish.
-Pour cream mixture over.
-Toss well.
-Sprinkle with parmesan.

FETTUCCINE AU FOUR

BAKED FETTUCCINE

Pasta and cheese are placed in a bread crumb lined dish and baked. Delicious.

1	lb	Fettuccine
7	tbs	Butter
1/4	cup	Parmesan cheese
1	cup	Heavy cream
1	lb	Fontina cheese cut in small pieces
		Black pepper
1/2	cup	Bread crumbs
1		Egg, beaten

-Boil fettuccine until al dente.
-Drain.
-Return to pot.
-Add 3 tbs butter, the parmesan, cream, Fontina and pepper to taste.
-Butter an oval casserole (9x14x2).
-Add 1/2 the bread crumbs and coat the caserole.
-Pour the egg into baking dish tilting to cover the crumbs.
-Add remaining crumbs and cover the egg.
-Transfer the fettuccine mixture to the casserole.
-Bake at 350 degrees for 15 minutes.
-Remove from the oven.
-Allow to rest for 10 minutes.
-Invert casserole onto a serving dish.
-Garnish with a tomato rose and parsley.

To BOIL means to cook food in liquid that maintains a temperature of 212 degrees. The liquid will bubble constantly and create steam.

SOUFFLE DE NOUILLES

PASTA SOUFFLE

Creamy and light is a souffle of pasta. It is unusual and delicious.

8	oz	Noodles, cooked and drained
3		Eggs, separated
1	stick	Melted butter
1	cup	Creamed cottage cheese
1	cup	Sour cream
1/2	cup	Soft bread crumbs
2	tbs	Butter cut in tiny pieces

-Beat egg yolks until light and lemon-yellow.
-Add melted butter and sugar.
-Mix well.
-Fold in the cottage cheese, sour cream and noodles.
-Beat egg whites until stiff and fold in.
-Butter a 2-quart casserole and pour in the mixture.
-Top with bread crumbs and bits of butter.
-Bake 45 minutes at 375 degrees.

To BEAT is the method whereby foods such as egg whites, cream are whipped vigorously with a wisk or electric mixer to incorporate small air bubbles into the mixture or whereby two or more ingredients are mixed together vigorously, such as egg yolks and sugar or butter, to form an homogenization of the ingredients.

GNOCCHI A LA ROMANO

GNOCCHI ROMAN STYLE

Gnocchi made from semolina or cream of farina is allowed to chill. It is then cut into three inch circles and baked with butter and parmesan cheese.

3	cups	Chicken stock
1/2	tsp	Salt
1/2	cup	Semolina or Cream of Farina
2	tbs	Butter
2/3	cup	Parmesan cheese
1/2	tsp	Dry mustard
1	tsp	Dijon mustard
		Cayenne pepper
2	tbs	Melted butter

-Place chicken stock and salt in a saucepan.
-Bring to a boil.
-Stir in semolina.
-Stir until it thickens.
-Remove from heat.
-Add butter, half the cheese, the two mustards and the cayenne.
-Cook 2 or 3 minutes over low heat.
-Spread mixture on a jelly roll pan to 1/2 inch thick.
-Chill until set.
-With a 1 1/2 inch round cookie cutter, cut pasta into rounds.
-Butter an oven proof dish.
-Arrange gnocchi slightly overlapping.
-Sprinkle with butter and rest of cheese.
-Brown under broiler.

SPAGHETTI CARUSO

SPAGHETTI WITH CHICKEN LIVERS

Onions, tomatoes and mushrooms are sauteed with chicken livers. A little white wine completes the sauce and the whole is served over boiled spaghetti.

1	cup	Onions, chopped
2	cloves	Garlic
4	tbs	Butter
4	tbs	Peanut oil
1	lb	Chicken livers
1	cup	Tomatoes, fresh and chopped
1	lb	Mushrooms, sliced
		Salt and pepper
1	cup	White wine

-Saute onions and garlic in butter for 3 minutes.
-Add oil.
-Add chicken livers and cook about 10 minutes.
-Add tomatoes and mushrooms and cook until chicken is done, about another 5 minutes.
-Salt and pepper.
-Add wine and simmer about 5 minutes.
-Serve over boiled spaghetti.

LASAGNA FRUITS DE MER

MIXED SEAFOOD LASAGNA

This variation of Italian lasagna layers broad noodles with shrimp, scallops, crab meat, ricotta cheese and a Veloute sauce. A welcome variation.

1	cup	Green onions, chopped
4	tbs	Butter
1/2	cup	White wine
1/2	lb	Shrimp (small)
1/2	lb	Scallops cut in small pieces
1/2	lb	Crab meat (dark)
1	cup	Mushrooms, sliced
4	tbs	Butter
4	tbs	Flour
		Salt and pepper
1	lb	Ricotta cheese
1	lb	Lasagna noodles, boiled as directed

-Saute green onions in butter.
-Add wine.
-Add shrimp and scallops.
-Cook 5 minutes.
-Add crab meat and mushrooms, salt and pepper.
-Strain, reserving both liquid and seafood.
-Melt butter in a saucepan.
-Add flour and cook 2 minutes.
-Add reserved poaching liquid.
-Cook until thickened.
-Salt and pepper.
-Set aside.
-Mix egg with ricotta cheese.
-In a buttered baking dish place a layer of lasagna noodles.
-Cover with a layer of ricotta cheese.
-Spread some of the seafood mixture over ricotta.
-Cover with a layer of the white sauce.
-Repeat layers of pasta, ricotta, seafood and white sauce until all is used.
-Finish with a layer of lasagna and top with a little white sauce.
-Bake in a 350 degree oven for 30 minutes.

PASTA A LA TERESA TURCI

PASTA WITH MEATBALLS, CHICKEN, AND MUSHROOMS

Madame Theresa Turci was the finest Italian chef I have ever known. She operated Turci's Italian restaurant for many years in New Orleans before her death. This was her specialty. A fantastic sauce on spaghetti topped with bite sized meat balls, boiled chicken and sauteed mushrooms.

1/3	cup	Olive oil
1	cup	Onions, chopped
1	cup	Celery, chopped
1	clove	Garlic, minced
1/2	cup	Ham and hamfat, diced
2	cups	Tomato paste
2	cups	Chicken stock
		Salt and pepper
2	cups	Ground meats, cooked 1/3 veal, 1/3 chicken gizzards, 1/3 pork (1/2 lb each)
2	cups	Chicken, boiled and sliced
2	cups	Meatballs, fried
2	cups	Sliced mushrooms

-Saute onions, celery and garlic in olive oil until soft.
-Add ham and hamfat.
-Add tomato paste, chicken broth, salt and pepper.
-Add ground meats.
-Let simmer 2 hours or longer.
-Strain.
-Add 10 minutes before serving the sliced chicken, meatballs and mushrooms.
-Serve on a bed of pasta.

NOUILLES SAUTEES CHOW MEIN

CHOW MEIN

This stir fry dish combines chicken, pork and shrimp with aromatic vegetables in a stock, sherry and soy sauce. Exceptionally good.

1/2	tbs	Sherry wine
1/2	tbs	Soy sauce
1	tsp	Cornstarch
4		Chicken breasts, deboned
1/2	lb	Pork, lean
2	tbs	Peanut oil
2	tbs	Ginger root, chopped
1	clove	Garlic,chopped
1/2	lb	Shrimp, cleaned
2		Onions, sliced
1		Green pepper, sliced
2	stalks	Celery, sliced
8		Green onions, chopped
1/4	lb	Cabbage, shredded
1/2	cup	Chicken stock
2	tsp	Cornstarch
1	tbs	Sherry
1	tbs	Soy sauce
1	recipe	Fried noodles

-Blend sherry, soy sauce and cornstarch in a large bowl.
-Cut chicken and pork into 1 inch pieces.
-Mix in cornstarch mixture.
-Heat oil in wok over high heat.
-Stir fry ginger and garlic 1 minute.
-Add chicken and pork and fry 5 minutes.
-Add shrimp and stir fry 3 minutes.
-Add onions, green pepper, celery, green onions and cabbage.
-Stir fry 3 minutes.
-Combine chicken stock, cornstarch, sherry and soy sauce.
-Pour over wok mixture.
-Stir cook until sauce thickens.
-Arrange noodles on serving plate.
-Arrange chow mein over noodles.

NOUILLES CHINOISE FRITES

FRIED CHINESE NOODLES (CHOW MEIN)

These home made chow mein noodles are so superior to the canned and they are fast and easy to make.

8	oz	Chinese noodles
		Water
		Salt
3	cups	Peanut oil

-Cook noodles in boiling salted water about 30 seconds.
-Drain.
-Arrange on towels to dry.
-Heat oil until 370 degrees.
-Fry noodles in small batches about 30 seconds.
-Drain on paper towels.

Desserts

Bill Hinton

DESSERTS

MOUSSE AU CHOCOLAT
CHOCOLATE MOUSSE

BLANC MANGE
CREOLE CUSTARD

MELANGE DES FRUITS CELESTINE
MIXED FRUIT CELESTINE

MACEDONIA INVERNALE
MARINATED DRIED AND FRESH FRUIT

GRATIN AUX FRIITS D'AUTOMNE
GRATIN OF AUTUMN FRUITS

FRAISES A LA BETE
STRAWBERRY FOOL

FRAISES MONSIEUR
STRAWBERRIES MISTER

POIRES AU GRATIN
BAKED PEARS

POIRES BELLE HELENE
ICE CREAM WITH PEARS AND CHOCOLATE SAUCE

POIRES A L'IMPERATRICE
PEARS WITH RICE CUSTARD

MADRILENES AU PECHE
PEACH MADRILENES

BANANES BAYOU LA FOURCHE
BANANA FRITTERS

TARTE ANTILLAISE AUX BANANES
BANANA TART

BUCHE DE NOEL
      CHRISTMAS LOG

CREME AU BEURRE
      BUTTER CREAM FROSTING

MERINGUE DE CHAMPIGNON
      MERINGUE MUSHROOM

GATEAU AU FROMAGE-CHOCOLAT ET FRAISES
      CHOCOLATE-STRAWBERRY CHEESECAKE

TORTE D'ORANGE ET CRANNEBERGES
      ORANGE CRANBERRY TORTE

GARNITURE
      TO GARNISH

ROULADE AUX NOIX CELEBRATION
      CELEBRATION PECAN ROULADE

TART AU NOIX ET FROMAGE BLANC
      PECAN CREAM CHEESE PIE

BEIGNETS CREOLE
      FRIED CORNMEAL CAKES

BISCUIT TORTONI
      ITALIAN ALMOND ICE CREAM

GLACE AU PETIT-LAIT
      BUTTERMILK ICE CREAM

GLACE A LA CANNELLE
      CINNAMON ICE CREAM

DESSERTS

One of the problems I have on Gourmet Cooking is to select dessert recipes which can be demonstrated quickly on a half-hour show along with two other recipes. This limits the choices since desserts usually require a lot of time and are frequently a combination of several recipes. One of the best quick desserts presented here is Strawberry Fool, simple, quick and delicious.

MOUSSE AU CHOCOLAT

CHOCOLATE MOUSSE

This classic French dessert is so easy to make and always welcome.

8	oz	Chocolate, semi-sweet
1/3	cup	Boiling water
2	tsp	Instant coffee
4		Egg yolks
2	tbs	Grand Marnier
4		Egg whites, beaten with...
3	tbs	Sugar

-In a food processor, chop chocolate pieces very fine.
-Dissolve instant coffee in boiling water.
-Add to chocolate.
-Process until smooth.
-Add egg yolks and Grand Marnier.
-Process until blended.
-Fold chocolate mixture into egg whites until completely blended.
-Spoon mousse into a serving bowl or into individual souffle cups.
-Chill 1 hour or more.
-Garnish with additional whipped cream if desired.

BLANC MANGE

CREOLE CUSTARD

My mother prepared this recipe often and a variation called Chocolate Blanc Mange. Substitute 4 oz semisweet chocolate for the orange zest and the almond extract.

1	qt	Milk
1/2	cup	Sugar
2		Eggs
		Zest of one lemon
1/2	cup	Cornstarch
1/8	tsp	Almond extract
1/4	tsp	Vanilla
4	tbs	Gelatin

-In a saucepan bring the milk to a boil.
-Blend together the sugar, egg and lemon zest.
-Mix cornstarch with additional milk.
-Add to hot milk.
-Add almond extract and vanilla.
-Cook until mixture thickens.
-Remove from the heat.
-Add the gelatin dissolved in a little water.
-Blend well.
-Strain into a mold or serving dish.
-Serve with fresh strawberries or other fresh fruit.

MELANGE DES FRUITS CELESTINE

MIXED FRUIT CELESTINE

Mixed fruits marinated in cherry flavored liquor fill scooped out pineapple shells for a taste treat that also pleases the eyes.

1		Pineapple	-Split pineapple lengthwise.
2		Oranges, peeled and sectioned	-Remove pineapple from shells and cut into
2		Bananas, cut into slices	bitesize pieces.
1	pt	Strawberries, halved	-Combine with other fruits.
1/2	lb	Seedless green grapes, halved	-Sprinkle with kirsch and sugar.
1/2	lb	Red grapes, seeded and halved	-Marinate covered for 30 minutes.
2		Golden delicious apples, peeled, cored and sliced	-Fill pineapple shells with fruit mixture and serve.
4	tbs	Kirsch	
4	tbs	Sugar	

FRAISES A LA BETE

STRAWBERRY FOOL

It is said that the name derives from the fact that any fool can make this dessert. Foolish or not, it is delicious and so easy to prepare. Other fruits can be substituted.

2	pkgs	Frozen strawberries	-Thaw strawberries.
1	cup	Almond macaroons, dry, crumbled	-Puree in a food processor. -Refrigerate.
2	cups	Cream, whipped	-Fold macaroons into whipped cream. -Partially blend cream into strawberries.

MACEDONIA INVERNALE

MARINATED DRIED AND FRESH FRUIT

Fresh fruit is combined with dried for a refreshing fruit dessert for the fall.

3/4	lb	Dried fruits, (figs, prunes, peach, apricots)	-Cut dried fruits into bite size pieces. -Steam over boiling water 10 to 15 minutes.
1		Lemon	-Grate rind from lemon and one orange into a
2		Oranges	bowl.
1	lg	Apple	-Peel and segment oranges.
1	lg	Pear	-Peel and core apple and pear.
2		Bananas	-Cut into bite size pieces.
1/4	cup	Sugar	-Slice banana.
2	tbs	Marischino liquor (optional)	-Mix all well. -Add sugar and optional marischino. -Cover and chill.

GRATIN AUX FRUITS D'AUTOMNE

GRATIN OF AUTUMN FRUITS

Taking advantage of the fruits of the season, this dessert bakes a taste treat which will create a great demand.

6		Eggs	-Break the eggs in a bowl.
1/2	cup	Sugar	-Add half the sugar and the cream.
1/2	cup	Cream	-Wisk mixture well.
3		Apples	-Peel the apples, pears, and bananas.
3		Pears	-Cut into bite size.
3		Bananas	-Place the apple juice in a skillet.
1/3	cup	Apple juice	-Add the remaining sugar and butter.
3	tbs	Apple brandy, (Calvados)	-Bring to a boil.
2	oz	Butter	-Add the fruits and cook 5 minutes.

-Remove the fruits with a skimmer and arrange them in a gratin dish.
-Pour the cooking juices into the egg/cream mixture.
-Pour the mixture over the fruits.
-Bake in a 375 degree oven for 15 minutes. minutes.
-Pour the apple brandy over and serve.

To FOLD is the technique of incorporating a dry mixture such as flour or a thick liquid mixture such as batter into another ingredient which has been BEATEN or WHIPPED without deflating the beaten ingredient. This is best done with a large spatula using strokes which go down the middle of the mixture to the bottom bringing some of the mixture up over the top while turning the bowl slightly with each stroke.

PATE AUX PECHES ET MYRTILLES

PEACH AND BLUEBERRY COBBLER

Peaches and blueberries combine with a rich batter to become an old fashioned southern dessert.

1	cup	Flour	-Blend together the flour, sugar, milk, baking powder and salt.
1	cup	Sugar	-Pour butter into a 3 quart baking pan.
3/4	cup	Milk	-Add batter to pan and mix well with butter.
1	tsp	Baking powder	-Mix peaches and blueberries together.
1/2	tsp	Salt	-Pour over batter.
1/2	cup	Butter, melted	-Bake at 350 degrees for 45 minutes until top is brown.
2	cups	Peaches, sliced	
1	cup	Blueberries	

FRAISES MONSIEUR

STRAWBERRIES MISTER

Whipped cream flavored with brown sugar gives this strawberry dessert a special character.

2	pts	Strawberries
1	cup	Heavy cream
4	tbs	Light brown sugar
1/2	tsp	Vanilla

-Clean, wash and hull strawberries.
-Whip cream until stiff.
-Sprinkle with brown sugar.
-Add vanilla.
-Mix well.
-Toss berries lightly in this mixture and chill until ready to serve.

POIRES AU GRATIN

BAKED PEARS

This simple dessert combines pears with apricot jam, wine and coconut cookies for a melange that will have your guests asking for more.

4-5		Pears
1	tbs	Butter
1/3	cup	Apricot jam
1/4	cup	Vermouth, dry
3-4		Macaroons, crumbled
2	tbs	Butter, cut into bits

-Butter a baking dish.
-Peel and core pears.
-Slice evenly, lengthwise.
-Mix jam with vermouth.
-Spread over pears.
-Crumble macaroons over pears.
-Dot with butter bits.
-Bake in a 350 degree oven for 20-25 minutes.

POIRES BELLE HELENE

ICE CREAM WITH PEARS AND CHOCOLATE SAUCE

A combination of three wonderful flavors, vanilla, pears and chocolate, make a simple but elegant dessert.

1	qt	Vanilla ice cream
12		Pear halves, canned
1	cup	Chocolate syrup

-Place ice cream in a mold and freeze.
-At serving time unmold on a serving dish.
-Surround with pear halves.
-Dribble some of the chocolate sauce over the ice cream.
-Serve the rest on the side.

POIRES A L'IMPERATRICE

PEARS WITH RICE CUSTARD

This dessert is fit for an empress as the name implies. A gelatinized rice custard with glaceed fruits is unmolded and surrounded by poached pears.

1/2	cup	Candied fruit, chopped	-Marinate fruit in liquor.
1/4	cup	Brandy or kirsch	-In a double boiler cook rice, milk and salt for
1/3	cup	Raw rice	1 hour.
4	cups	Milk	-In a large bowl combine milk, eggs, sugar
1	tsp	Salt	and vanilla.
1	tsp	Vanilla	-Blend in rice and milk.
1	tbs	Lemon juice	-Add candied fruit.
2	tbs	Gelatin, unflavored	-Add gelatin soaked in lemon juice.
1	cup	Milk	-Pour into a 2 quart mold.
3		Eggs	-Set in pan of water.
3/4	cup	Sugar	-Bake uncovered for 60 minutes.
4		Pears	-Refrigerate until cool.
1 1/2	cups	Water	-Peel pears and halve.
3/4	cup	Sugar	-Boil sugar, water and vanilla 5 minutes.
1	tsp	Vanilla	-Add pears and simmer covered for about 10
1		Lemon juice	minutes.
			-Cool.
			-Unmold rice custard.
			-Surround with pears and some of the syrup.

One cup heavy cream yields 2 cups whipped.

MADRILENES AU PECHE

PEACH MADRILENES

Peach halves filled with grapes and orange segments blended into whipped cream creates a refreshing and easy dessert.

24		Green grapes	-Halve and deseed grapes.
2		Oranges	-Segment oranges.
1	cup	Heavy cream	-Whip cream.
2	tsp	Sugar	-Add sugar.
8	lg	Peach halves	-Add grapes and oranges.
			-Pile into the peach halves.

BANANES BAYOU LA FOURCHE

BANANA FRITTERS

Firm bananas dipped in a thick batter are deep fried to make a wonderful cajun dessert.

4		Bananas, cut in one inch pieces
1 1/2	cups	Flour
2	tsp	Baking powder
1/2	tsp	Salt
1	tbs	Sugar
2		Eggs, beaten
		Vegetable oil, 2 inches deep in pan

-Mix the dry ingredients, pour beaten eggs into a hole in center and gradually blend into a batter.
-Add a little milk if needed: you want a thick batter.
-Dip banana pieces in batter and drop immediately into hot oil.
-Fry until golden brown.
-Makes about 2 1/2 dozen.
-You may also use apple slices, if you wish.

To BLEND means to mix together several ingredients without BEATING so as to evenly dispurse the individual item.

TARTE ANTILLAISE AUX BANANES

BANANA TART

A sweet pastry dough is filled with a pastry cream covered with banana slices and glazed with a pineapple sauce.

1	recipe	Pate sucree
2/3	cup	Sugar
2/3	cup	Water
6	tbs	Rum
5		Bananas
1 1/2	cups	Pastry cream
2 3/4	cups	Pineapple
1/2	cup	Sugar

-Roll dough to line a 10 1/2 inch pie pan.
-Preheat oven to 425 degrees.
-Mix sugar, water and rum in a large skillet.
-Bring to a boil.
-Peel bananas and cut into 1/2 inch slices.
-Place in syrup-rum mixture.
-Simmer for 10 minutes, set aside.
-Prick dough, line with foil and fill with beans.
-Bake at 425 degrees for 25 minutes.
-Fill cooked pie crust with pastry cream.
-Cover with banana slices.
-In a blender, blend pineapple and sugar.
-Cover bananas with pineapple sauce.

BUCHE DE NOEL

CHRISTMAS LOG

A Christmas log is a classic French dessert prepared during the Christmas season. We prepared it on our one hour Christmas special show.

4	lg	Eggs
1	cup	Sugar
5	tbs	Water
1 1/2	tsp	Vanilla
1	cup	Cake flour, sifted
1/4	tsp	Salt
1	tsp	Baking powder
1	recipe	Butter cream
1/3	cup	Grand Marnier
1 1/2	cup	Orange marmalade
		Confectioners sugar

-Line a greased 10x15 inch jelly roll pan with waxed paper.
-Grease waxed paper.
-Beat eggs until thick.
-Gradually beat in sugar.
-Add water.
-Add flour, salt and baking powder.
-Pour batter into jelly roll pan.
-Bake in a 375 degree oven for 15 minutes.
-Turn out of pan onto a tea towel.
-Roll towel and cake together.
-Cool.
-Unroll cake and sprinkle with Grand Marnier.
-Cover with orange marmalade.
-Roll cake in jelly roll fashion.
-Cut ends off diagonally and set aside.
-Spread butter over outside of roll.
-Place cut pieces onto roll to resemble stumps of a log.
-Spread frosting over stumps.
-Run tines of a fork down the length of the roll to simulate bark.
-Garnish with meringue mushrooms and chocolate leaves.
-Sprinkle with confectioner's sugar to simulate snow.
-NOTE: Must be refrigerated to keep butter cream firm.

CREME AU BEURRE

BUTTER CREAM FROSTING

1/2	cup	Sugar
1/8	tsp	Cream of tartar
2	tbs	Water
3		Egg yolks
1	lb	Butter
1	tsp	Vanilla
1	tsp	Instant coffee dissolved in the vanilla
3	tbs	Cocoa

-Combine sugar, cream of tartar and water.
-Bring to a boil, stirring constantly until a thick syrup.
-Cool about 1 minute.
-Beat egg yolks until very thick.
-Gradually beat in syrup.
-Beat in butter 2 to 3 tablespoons at a time.
-Add vanilla/coffee mixture.
-Add cocoa.
-Beat until well blended.
-Chill until firm but spreadable.

MERINGUE DE CHAMPIGNON

MERINGUE MUSHROOM

These confections, while intended as a garnish to the Buche de Noel are delicious in themselves. I place them in crates or boxes wrapped in plastic wrap. They truly look like mushrooms.

4		Egg whites
1	cup	Sugar
		Cocoa

-Beat egg whites on medium speed.
-When whites are very foamy, gradually add sugar.
-Beat until very stiff.
-Fill a pastry bag with meringue.
-Pipe out mushroom caps and stems onto cookie sheet covered with parchment paper.
-Bake in a 275 degree oven for 40 to 50 minutes.
-Remove and cool.
-Cut a small hole in the bottom of each mushroom cap.
-Dip the top of each stem in uncooked meringue.
-Insert into hole in cap.

All utensils should be clean and dry and free from any fats when beating egg whites.

GATEAU AU FROMAGE - CHOCOLAT ET FRAISES

CHOCOLATE-STRAWBERRY CHEESECAKE

Our one hour Easter special featured this delicious cheesecake garnished with strawberries.

2	cups	Chocolate wafers
1/3	cup	Sugar
6	tbs	Butter
2	lbs	Cream cheese
1 1/2	cups	Sugar
3	tbs	Flour
1 1/2	tsp	Orange zest
1	tsp	Vanilla
5		Eggs
1		Egg yolk
1/3	cup	Cream
1	cup	Sour Cream
1	tbs	Sugar
1	tsp	Vanilla
2	pts	Strawberries
3/4	cup	Red currant jelly

-Crush chocolate wafers very fine.
-Add sugar and butter and combine well.
-Butter a 10 inch springform pan.
-Press mixture onto bottom and sides of pan.
-Blend together the cream cheese, sugar, flour, orange zest, vanilla, eggs and cream.
-Pour into the pan.
-Bake at 325 degrees for 1 hour.
-Turn oven off.
-Let cake rest in the closed oven for one hour.
-Blend sour cream, sugar and vanilla.
-Spread on top of cake.
-Bake 5 minutes.
-Cool, then refrigerate.
-Heat current jelly until melted.
-Glaze berries with jelly.
-Arrange berries on top of the cake with the tips up.

TORTE D'ORANGE ET CRANNEBERGES

ORANGE CRANBERRY TORTE

One of the most popular desserts I prepare. A must at Thanksgiving and Christmas. I prepared it for the one hour Thanksgiving show.

2 1/4	cups	Flour
1	cup	Sugar
1/4	tsp	Salt
1	tsp	Baking powder
1	cup	Pecans, chopped
1	cup	Dates, chopped
1	cup	Cranberries
1	tsp	Baking soda
2	tbs	Orange zest
2		Eggs, beaten
1	cup	Buttermilk
3/4	cup	Salad oil
1	cup	Orange juice
1	cup	Sugar

-Sift together flour, sugar, salt, baking powder and soda.
-Stir in nuts, dates, cranberries and orange zest.
-Combine eggs, buttermilk and salad oil in a separate bowl.
-Add to flour and fruit mixture.
-Blend well.
-Pour into a well greased bundt mold or tube baking pan.
-Bake one hour at 350 degrees.
-Remove from oven, cool in pan.
-Remove from pan to cake dish.
-Combine orange juice and sugar.
-Bring to a boil.
-Pour over cake.
-Wrap in aluminum foil and refrigerate at least two hours.

GARNITURE

TO GARNISH

1 1/2	cups	Kumquarts, preserved
1 1/2	cups	Pecans, whole halves
1 1/2	cups	Cranberries
1 1/2	cups	Dates, whole and pitted
1 1/2	cups	Orange juice
3/4	cup	Sugar
1	tbs	Cornstarch
1	tbs	Water
		Ivy leaves

-Add orange juice and sugar together in a saucepan.
-Bring to a boil and cook until sugar is completely dissolved.
-Blend cornstarch and water together.
-Add to orange sugar mixture.
-Cook until mixture is slightly thickened.
-Remove from the heat.
-Arrange pecans, cranberries and dates on individual plates.
-Pour three or four tablespoons over each.
-Toss each ingredient to glaze.
-Glaze ivy leaves by dipping in sugar mixture.
-Place cake on a cake plate or stand.
-Arrange some kumquarts, pecans, cranberries and dates in the center of the cake.
-Arrange in clusters around base of cake the kumquarts, pecans, cranberries and dates in that order.
-Place ivy leaves in and among the fruits and nuts in a decorative manner.

ROULADE AUX NOIX CELEBRATION

CELEBRATION PECAN ROULADE

This spectacular cake was prepared for one one-hour special Fourth of July show. It was presented with three sparklers glowing.

6		Egg yolks
3/4	cup	Sugar
1 1/2	cups	Pecans, chopped
1	tbs	Baking powder
6		Egg whites
2	cups	Cream
1/4	cup	Confectioner's sugar
1/2	tsp	Vanilla
1	cup	Strawberries
1	cup	Blueberries

-Line a jelly roll pan with wax paper.
-Butter generously.
-Blend yolks and sugar until thick and light yellow.
-Add pecans and baking powder.
-Beat egg whites until stiff.
-Fold into the yolk mixture.
-Pour into the jelly roll pan.
-Bake at 350 degrees for 20 minutes.
-Remove from oven.
-Turn upside down on a clean dishtowel.
-Remove pan and wax paper.
-Roll in towel while hot.
-Set aside to cool.
-Whip cream until firm.
-Blend in confectioner's sugar and vanilla.
-Unroll cake.
-Spread some of the cream on cake.
-Spread some of both the berries over cream.
-Roll cake.
-Place on a serving dish seam side down.
-Cover cake with more whipped cream.
-Place remaining cream in a pastry bag with a large star tip.
-On the diagonal across the cake pipe a row of cream.
-On one side of row place a row of strawberries and on other a row of blueberries.
-Repeat until whole cake is covered.
-Pipe remaining cream around cake and garnish with additional berries.
-Refrigerate.
-At serving time light three sparklers and insert into cake.

One pound granulated sugar equals 2 cups.

TART AU NOIX ET FROMAGE BLANC

PECAN CREAM CHEESE PIE

Cream cheese cuts the clawing sweetness most pecan pies have and adds a creamy texture for a dessert you will repeat over and over.

8	oz	Cream cheese
4		Eggs
6	tbs	Sugar
2	tsp	Vanilla
3/4	cup	Corn syrup
3	oz	Pecans, chopped
1	9 in	Pastry shell

-Soften cream cheese to room temperature.
-Cream together with 1 egg, 4 tablespoons sugar and 1 teaspoon vanilla.
-In another bowl beat together corn syrup, 1 teaspoon vanilla, 3 eggs and 2 tablespoons sugar.
-Pour cream cheese mixture into pie shell.
-Spread chopped pecans over cheese.
-Pour second mixture over pecans.
-Bake at 375 for 35 minutes.

When measuring syrups or other liquids which tend to cling, lightly butter the measuring cup or spoon.

BEIGNETS CREOLE

FRIED CORNMEAL CAKES

Sometimes called cajun doughnuts, this cornmeal batter puffs up and becomes light and airy when deep fried.

1	cup	White cornmeal
1	cup	Water, boiling
1		Egg, beaten
1	tbs	Peanut oil
1	tbs	Sugar
3/4	tsp	Salt
1/2	tsp	Baking powder
3/4	cup	Milk
1	cup	Self rising flour

-Mix cornmeal and water together.
-Let cool.
-Add egg, oil, sugar, salt, baking powder, milk and flour.
-Blend well.
-Drop by tablespoons in deep hot oil until they brown and rise to the top.
-Drain.

BISCUIT TORTONI

ITALIAN ALMOND ICE CREAM

Almonds and sherry wine combine to give this light Italian ice cream its unique flavor.

2	tbs	Water
1/3	cup	Sugar
3		Egg yolks
2	tbs	Sherry, dry
1	cup	Cream, whipped until stiff
1/3	cup	Almonds, toasted and finely ground

-Bring sugar and water to a boil and cook for 3 minutes.
-Blend together the egg yolks and sherry.
-Wisk in the sugar syrup.
-Fold the sugar mixture into the whipped cream.
-Pour into 8 paper muffin cups in a muffin tin.
-Sprinkle with ground nuts.
-Freeze for 4 to 5 hours.

GLACE AU PETIT-LAIT

BUTTERMILK ICE CREAM

Mrs. Sis Lipson provided me with this very old recipe for Buttermilk ice cream as it was served by a now closed Pensacola ice cream parlor.

1	qt	Buttermilk
1/2	pt	Cream
1	can	Condensed milk (15 oz)
1	can	Evaporated milk (13 oz)
1/2	cup	Lemon juice
1/2	cup	Sugar

-Combine buttermilk, cream, milks, vanilla, lemon juice and sugar.
-Place in ice cream freezer can and freeze according to directions.
-Optional: Replace part or all the lemon juice

GLACE A LA CANNELLE

CINNAMON ICE CREAM

Unusual and delicious is this old Pensacola recipe for cinnamon ice cream. This recipe came to me through the collection of Mrs. Sis Lipson.

1	cup	Sugar
6	tbs	Water
1 1/2	tbs	Cinnamon
3	cups	Milk, scalded
3/4	cups	Sugar
1		Egg yolk, beaten
2	cups	Cream
1	tsp	Vanilla

-Combine sugar, water and cinnamon.
-Cook over low heat until sugar is dissolved.
-Set aside.
-Blend sugar into scalded milk.
-Add egg yolk.
-Cook over low heat, stirring, until slightly thickened.
-Add the cinnamon syrup, cream and vanilla.
-Pour into an ice cream freezer and freeze according to directions.
-Let rest for several hours to mellow.

Breads

BREADS

PAIN FRANCAIS
FRENCH BREAD

PAIN BIS
WHOLE WHEAT BREAD

PAIN DE SEIGLE
RYE BREAD

PAIN DE SEIGLE DE BRASSEUR
BREWER'S RYE BREAD

PAIN NOIR AU RUSSE
RUSSIAN BLACK BREAD

PAINS DE POMME DE TERRE
POTATO LOAVES

BISCUITS DUR
HARD-TACK

BREADS

Bread making is one of the most rewarding chores one can do in the kitchen. There seems to something theraputic about kneading dough. The fragrance of yeast risen dough baking in the oven is one of life's pleasures. We present here some recipes for some wonderful breads which will enhance any meal.

PAIN FRANCAIS

FRENCH BREAD

This recipe and the next five were demonstrated by a very talented teacher Mrs. Norma Murray in cooking classes at The Kitchen Shoppe in Pensacola. I have used them many times and they are excellent.

6	cups	White flour
2	pkgs	Active dry yeast
1	tbs	Sugar
2	tbs	Shortening
2	tsp	Salt
2 1/4	cups	Hot water
1-2	tbs	Oil

-Combine 2 cups flour, undissolved yeast, sugar and salt in a large bowl.
-Stir well to blend.
-Add shortening then hot water (115-120) degrees).
-Beat with electric mixer at medium speed for 3-4 minutes.
-Add one cup more flour and beat at high speed until well blended.
-Gradually stir in enough additional flour to make a soft dough which leaves the side of the bowl.
-Turn out onto a floured board and knead until smooth and elastic.
-Cover with plastic wrap, then a towel.
-Let rest until doubled in bulk.
-Punch dough down and divide in half.
-Roll each half into an 8x15 in. rectangle.
-Roll up tightly beginning with the long side.
-Seal all edges well.
-Place seamside down on greased baking sheets.
-Brush dough lightly with oil.
-Cover baking sheet loosely with plastic wrap until loaves are doubled in bulk.
-Brush loaves lightly with cold water just before baking.
-Bake at 375-400 degrees about 35-40 minutes.
-Bread will sound hollow when tapped.
-Remove from sheets and cool on wire racks.

PAIN BIS

WHOLE WHEAT BREAD

5	cups	White flour
3	cups	Whole wheat flour
3	tbs	Sugar
1	tbs	Salt
2	pkgs	Active dry yeast
2	cups	Milk
3/4	cup	Water
1/4	cup	Margarine

-Combine flours.
-In a large bowl, thoroughly mix 2 1/2 cups flour mixture, sugar, salt and undissolved yeast.
-Combine milk, water and margarine in a saucepan.
-Heat over low heat until liquids are very warm (115-120 degrees).
-Gradually add to dry ingredients and beat 3 to 4 minutes at medium speed of electric mixer.
-Add one cup flour mixture.
-Beat at high speed until well blended.
-Stir in enough additional flour mixture to make a stiff dough.
-Turn out onto a lightly floured board and knead until smooth and elastic.
-Cover with plastic wrap, then a towel.
-Let rest until doubled in bulk.
-Divide dough in half.
-Punch down and shape into loaves.
-Place in greased loaf pans.
-Cover with plastic wrap and let rise until bread comes to the top of the pan.
-Puncture any gas bubble which may have formed with a greased toothpick.
-Bake at 350 degrees about 40 minutes.
-Bread will sound hollow when tapped.
-Remove from pans and cool on wire racks.

PAIN DE SEIGLE

RYE BREAD

4	cups	White flour
2	cups	Medium rye flour
1/2	tbs	Salt
1	tbs	Caraway seed
2	pkgs	Active dry yeast
1/4	cup	Softened margarine
2	cups	Very warm water
1/3	cup	Molasses

-Combine flours.
-In a large bowl, thoroughly mix 2 cups flour mixture, salt, caraway seed and undissolved yeast.
-Add margarine and mix well.
-Gradually add water and molasses to dry ingredients and beat 3-4 minutes at medium speed of electric mixer.
-Add one cup more flour mixture and beat at high speed 3-4 minutes.
-Stir in enough additional flour mixture to make a stiff dough.
-Turn out onto a floured board and knead until smooth and elastic.
-Cover with plastic wrap, then a towel.
-Let rise in warm, draft-free place until doubled in bulk.
-Punch dough down and divide in half.
-Form each half into a smooth, round ball.
-Flatten each ball into a mound 7 inches in diameter.
-Place in greased cake pan and let rise until doubled in bulk.
-Bake at 350 degrees about 35-40 minutes.
-Bread will sound hollow when tapped.
-Remove from pan and cool on wire racks.

PAIN DE SEIGLE DE BRASSEUR

BREWER'S RYE BREAD

5	cups	White flour
4	cups	Rye flour
2	cups	Milk
1	tbs	Salt
1/3	cup	Dark molasses
1/4	cup	Margarine
1 1/2	cups	Beer
2	pkgs	Yeast
1/2	tsp	Fennel seed

-Combine flours and set aside.
-In a large bowl, thoroughly mix 2 cups flour mixture, salt, yeast and fennel seed.
-Combine milk, molases, margarine and beer in saucepan.
-Heat over low heat until liquids are very warm (120-130 degrees).
-Gradually add to dry ingredients and beat 2 minutes at medium speed of electric mixer.
-Add additional flour mixture to make a stiff dough.
-Turn out onto a lightly floured board.
-Knead until smooth and elastic.
-Place in a greased bowl, turning to grease top.
-Cover with plastic wrap.
-Let rise in warm, draft-free place until doubled in bulk, about 1 hour.
-Punch dough down and divide in half.
-Form each half into a smooth round ball.
-Flatten each ball into a mound, about 7 inches in diameter.
-Place in greased 8 or 9 inch cake pans.
-Cover with plastic wrap; let rise in warm, draft-free place until doubled in bulk.
-Bake at 350 degrees 35-40 minutes.
-Remove from baking pans and cool on wire racks.

PAIN NOIR AU RUSSE

4	cups	Rye flour
3	cups	White flour
2	tsp	Sugar
2	tsp	Salt
2	cups	Whole bran cereal
2	tbs	Caraway seed
2	tsp	Instant coffee
1	tsp	Onion powder
1/2	tsp	Fennel seed .
2	pkgs	Yeast
2 1/2	cups	Water
1/4	cup	Vinegar
1/4	cup	Dark molasses
1	square	
	(1oz)	Unsweetened chocolate
1/4	cup	Margarine
1	tsp	Cornstarch
1/2	cup	Cold water

-Combine flours. In a large bowl, thoroughly mix 2 cups flour mixture, sugar, salt, cereal, caraway seed, instant coffee, onion powder, fennel seed and yeast.
-Combine 2 1/2 cups water, vinegar, molasses, chocolate and margarine in saucepan.
-Heat over low heat until liquids are very warm (120-130 degrees).
-Gradually add to dry ingredients and beat 2 minutes at medium speed of electric mixer.
-Add additional flour mixture to make a soft dough that leaves the side of the bowl.
-Turn out onto a lightly floured board.
-Knead until smooth and elastic (dough may be sticky).
-Place in a greased bowl, turning to grease top.
-Cover with plastic wrap.
-Let rise in warm, draft-free place until doubled in bulk.
-Punch dough down and divide in half.
-Shape each half into a smooth, round ball.
-Flatten each ball into a mound, about 7 inches in diameter.
-Place in greased 8 or 9 inch round cake pan.
-Cover with plastic wrap and let rise in warm, draft-free place until doubled in bulk.
-Bake at 350 degrees 45-50 minutes.
-Meanwhile, combine cornstarch and cold water.
-Cook over medium heat, stirring constantly until mixture starts to boil and continue to cook for 1 minute.
-As soon as bread is baked, brush cornstarch mixture over top of loaves.
-Return bread to oven and bake 2-3 minutes longer, or until glaze is set.
-Remove from pans and cool on wire racks.

PAINS DE POMME DE TERRE

POTATO LOAVES

1	lg	Potato
2	pkgs	Yeast
2	tbs	Margarine
2	tbs	Sugar
1	tbs	Salt
1	cup	Milk
7	cups	Flour

-Peel and dice potato.
-Boil in water to cover until tender.
-Drain, reserving liquid.
-Add water to potato liquid to make 1 cup.
-Set aside.
-Mash potato and set aside.
-In a large bowl, thoroughly mix 2 cups flour, salt and yeast.
-Combine milk, potato liquid and margarine in saucepan.
-Heat over low heat until liquids are very warm (120-130 degrees).
-Gradually add to dry ingredients and beat 2 minutes at medium speed of electric mixer.
-Add potato.
-Add additional flour to make a stiff dough.
-Turn out onto a lightly floured board.
-Knead until smooth and elastic.
-Place in greased bowl, turning to grease top.
-Cover with plastic wrap.
-Let rise in warm, draft-free place, until doubled in bulk.
-Punch dough down and turn over in bowl.
-Cover with plastic wrap and let rise again about 20 minutes.
-Punch dough down and divide in half.
-Roll each half to a 9x14 inch rectangle.
-Shape into loaves.
-Place in 2 greased loaf pans.
-Cover with plastic wrap.
-Let rise in warm, draft-free place until doubled in bulk.
-Dust loaves with flour.
-Bake at 350 degrees 35-40 minutes.
-Remove from pans and cool on wire racks.

BISCUITS DUR

A very hard bread or biscuit that was referred to as sea biscuit many years ago when it was used for long voyages at sea. It was softened with a liquid such as soup. This practice of dipping hard tack into Gaspacio soup by the Spanish is believed to have been the origin of Gaspache salad (Volume I).

4	cups	Flour,sifted
1	pkg	Yeast
1	cup	Water
1/2	tsp	Salt

-Proof yeast in 1/3 cup of warm water (110 115 degrees).

-Blend flour, salt, yeast and remaining water to form a stiff dough.

-Knead for 10 minutes.

-Place in a greased bowl and cover.

-Let rise till double (about 45 to 60 minutes).

-Punch down and knead another 5 minutes.

-Roll dough to a thickness of 1/2 inch.

-Cut into round biscuits about 5 inches round.

-Prick with a fork several times on top.

-Bake at 300 degrees for one hour.

-Reduce heat to 250 degrees and bake another hour.

-Reduce heat a third time to 200 degrees and bake another hour.

-Turn heat off.

-Allow oven to cool.

-Remove biscuits from oven and let them cool completely.

-Store in air tight containers.

-They will last for several years.

-To use: crush with a mallet and soak with a liquid such as vinaigrette sauce in the Gaspache Salad in Volume I.

NOTES

Index of TV Shows

SHOW 144
TRUITE AMANDINE
TROUT ALMMONDINE
POMMES DE TERRE ANNA
BAKED POTATO CAKE

SHOW 145
COTE DE PORC SAUCE DIABLE
SAUTEED PORK FILETS - DEVIL SAUCE
SALADE DE CHOUCROUTE ET POMMES
CABBAGE AND APPLE SALAD

SHOW 146
JAMBONETTES DE VOLAILLE
STUFFED CHICKEN LEGS
OIGNONS ET CAROTTES A LA GRECQUE
GREEK STYLE ONIONS AND CARROTS

SHOW 147
POULET EN BROCHETTE AUX BEURRE ANCHOIS
SKEWERED CHICKEN - ANCHOVY BUTTER
LA SPADELLATA
SPAGHETTI IN CREAM-TOMATO SAUCE
MACEDOMIA INVERNALE
MARINATED DRIED AND FRESH FRUITS

SHOW 148
CREVETTES ET CHAMPIGNONS - SAUCE ANETH
SHRIMP AND MUSHROOMS IN DILL SAUCE
SALADE DE BROCOLI
BROCCOLI SALAD
SAUCE CREOLE
CREOLE DRESSING

SHOW 149
COTE DE PORC AU CERISES
PORK CHOPS WITH CHERRIES
SALADE DE CRUDITES
VEGETABLE SALAD

SHOW 150
SUPREMES DE VOLAILLE A LA MARSALA
SAUTEED CHICKEN BREASTS WITH MARSALA WINE SAUCE
FETTUCCINI AU FOUR
BAKED FETTUCCINI
PECHES EPICES
SPICED PEACHES

SHOW 151
CHAMPIGNONS A L'AIOLI
MUSHROOMS WITH GARLIC MAYONNAISE
TRUITE VIENNOISE
TROUT IN RED WINE SAUCE
RIZ AU CITRON
LEMON RICE WITH GREEN PEAS

SHOW 152
SAUTE DE CRABE FINE BOUCHE
SAUTEED LUMP CRAB GOURMET
NOUILLES VERTS A LA MAISON
GREEN NOODLES WITH PEAS
POIRES AU GRATIN
BAKED PEARS

SHOW 153
BOEUF FARCI A LA SAUCE HUITRES
STUFFED FLANK WITH OYSTER SAUCE
SAUCE D'HUITRES
OYSTER SAUCE
SALADE PASTA PRIMAVERA
PASTA PRIMAVERA SALAD

SHOW 154
CROQUETTES DE SAUMON
SALMON CROQUETTES
SAUCE CITRON AUX CAPRES
LEMON CAPER SAUCE
NOUILLES ET PETIT POIS
BUTTERED NOODLES AND GREEN PEAS
FRAISES A LA BETE
STRAWBERRY FOOL

SHOW 155
POULET A LA TETRAZZINI
CHICKEN TETRAZZINI
SALADE DES EPINARDS ET DES TOMATES
SPINACH AND TOMATO SALAD WITH HORSERADISH CREAM DRESSING

SHOW 156
TRANCHES DE JAMBON FINES BOUCHES
HAM STEAKS GOURMET
SALADE DE COURGETTES ET DE CHAMPIGNONS
ZUCCHINI AND MUSHROOM SALAD
SAUCE VINAIGRETTE
VINAIGRETTE SAUCE

SHOW 157
ETOUFEE DES ECREVESSE
CRAWFISH ETOUFEE
FUMET DE ECREVESSE
CRAWFISH STOCK

SHOW 158
SUPREMES DE VOLAILLES QUARTRE SAISONS
SAUTEED CHICKEN BREASTS FOUR SEASONS
COURGETTES NICOISE
ZUCCHINI NICOISE
FRAISES MONSIEUR
STRAWBERRIES MISTER

SHOW 159
CREVETTES ET HUITRES CREOLE
SHRIMP AND OYSTER CREOLE
SALADE AU BROCOLI EN ROND
BROCCOLI SALAD RING
SAUCE VINAIGRETTE
VINAIGRETTE SAUCE

SHOW 160
BLANC DE VOLAILLE MEDITERRANEE
CHICKEN BREASTS MEDITERRANEAN
SALADE DE PAMPLEMOUSSE ET CONCOMBRE
GRAPEFRUIT AND CUCUMBER SALAD
MOUSSE AU CHOCOLATE
CHOCOLATE MOUSSE

SHOW 161
COTES DES CRABES
CRAB CHOPS
BLANC MANGE
CREOLE CUSTARD
TOMATES FARCIES AVEC BROCOLI
TOMATOES STUFFED WITH BROCCOLI

SHOW 162
OEUFS SAINT LOUIS
EGGS SAINT LOUIS
OEUFS POCHES
POACHED EGGS
SALADE DES GOMBOS ET TOMATES
OKRA AND TOMATO SALAD
SALADE VERT-SAUCE CREOLE
CREOLE SALAD

SHOW 163
FILETS DES FLOUNDER PARISIENNE
SHRIMP STUFFED FLOUNDER FILETS
POMME DE TERRE DUCHESSE
DUCHESSE POTATOES
POIRES BELLE HELENE
ICE CREAM WITH PEARS AND CHOCOLATE SAUCE

SHOW 164
TRANCHES DE JAMBON ROULE AUX PECHES
HAM ROLLS WITH PEACHES
RIZ AMANDINE AVEC CHAMPIGNONS
ALMOND RICE WITH MUSHROOMS
SALADE MELANGEE AUX FROMAGE BLEU
MIXED SALAD WITH BLUE CHEESE

SHOW 165
CHOU FARCI A LA NICOISE
STUFFED CABBAGE NICOISE
POMMES AU POIVREES
PEPPERED APPLES
SAUCE TOMATE
TOMATO SAUCE

SHOW 166

CREVETTES A LA ROCKERFELLER
SHRIMP ROCKERFELLER
CREVETTES BOUILLI
BOILED SHRIMP
SALADE DE BETTERAVES AUX NOIX
BEET AND WALNUT SALAD
GRATIN AUX FRIITS D'AUTOMNE
GRATIN OF AUTUMN FRUITS

SHOW 167

AVACAT AU PAMPLEMOUSSE
AVOCADO AND GRAPEFRUIT SALAD
SAUCE VINAIGRETTE
VINAIGRETTE SAUCE
POULET UN DEUX TROIS
CHICKEN ONE TWO THREE
SAUCE UN DEUX TROIS
SAUCE ONE TWO THREE

SHOW168

CREVETTES ETOUFEE
SHRIMP STEW
PATE AUX PECHES ET MYRTILLES
PEACH AND BLUEBERRY COBBLER
SALADE DE LEGUMES VERTS
GREEN VEGETABLE SALAD

SHOW 169

SAUTE DE POULET AUX CHAMPIGNONS
CHICKEN AND MUSHROOMS IN CREAM SAUCE
SALADE TOMATE SAUCE CREOLE
TOMATO SALAD SAUCE CREOLE

SHOW 170

BOULETTES DE VIANDE A L'ITALIENNE
VEAL MEATBALLS ITALIAN STYLE
BISCUIT TORTONI
ITALIAN ICE CREAM

SHOW 171
CREVETTES A LA TETRAZZINI
SHRIMP TETRAZZINI
SALADE DES HARICOTS VERTS
MARINATED GREEN BEAN SALAD

SHOW 172
VELOUTE D'OIGNON
CREAM OF ONION SOUP
POULET EN CASSEROLE
CHICKEN SUPREME

SHOW 173
CROQUETTES DE BOEUF EN SAUCE TOMATE
BEEF CROQUETTES IN TOMATO SAUCE
POMMES DE TERRE AU FOUR GALANTE
ELEGANT BAKED POTATOES

SHOW 174
CASSEROLE DE CHAIR DE CRABE
CRAB MEAT CASSEROLE
SALADE DE POMMES DE TERRE SUISSE
SWISS POTATO SALAD

SHOW 175
COTE DE PORC AUX POMMES
PORK CHOPS WITH APPLES
NOUILLES A L'ALLEMAGNE
GERMAN NOODLES

SHOW 176
CHAIR DE CRABE CHANDELEUR
CRAB MEAT FEAST OF CANDLEMAS
COURGETTES NICOISE
ZUCCHINI NICOISE

SHOW 177
√ RAGOUT DE BOEUF A LA GRECQUE
BEEF STEW GREEK STYLE
OIGNONS AU FOUR
ROASTED ONIONS

Broccoli + mushroom salad
w/ mustard mayo

SHOW 178
CREVETTES FARCIES HOLLANDAISE
STUFFED SHRIMP HOLLANDAISE
FARCI DE CHAIR DE CRABE
CRAB MEAT STUFFING

SHOW 179 ✓
POULET AUX PAPRIKA
CHICKEN PAPRIKA
CHOU CHINOIS AUX CHAMPIGNONS
CHINESE CABBAGE WITH MUSHROOMS

SHOW 180
CREPES FARCIES FORESTIERE
HAM EGG AND MUSHROOM CREPES
SALADE AU PERSIL
PARSLEY SALAD

SHOW 181 ✓
DAUBE DE PORC AUX POIVRONS *103*
BRAISED PORK AND PEPPERS WITH NOODLES
SOUPE VERTE *69*
GREEN VEGETABLE SOUP
Orange Salad

SHOW 182
HUITRES AUX CARPES
OYSTERS IN CAPER SAUCE
MADRILENES AU PECHE
PEACHES MADRILENES
Russian Salad

SHOW 183
HAMBURGERS A LA CREME D'OIGNONS
HAMBURGERS WITH CREAMED ONIONS
SALADE A LA MAISON
GREEN HOUSE SALAD

SHOW 184
POULET SAUCE PIQUANT
CHICKEN SAUCE PIQUANT
RIZ BOUILLI
BOILED RICE
BANANES BAYOU LA FOURCHE
BANANA FRITTERS

SHOW 185
BOEUF AU POIVRON ET AUX CHAMPIGNONS
BRAISED BEEF PEPPERS AND MUSHROOMS
SALADE DE CHOU ROUGE ET ANANAS
RED CABBAGE AND PINEAPPLE SALAD

SHOW 186
LASAGNE FRUITS DE MER
MIXED SEAFOOD LASAGNA
SALADE DE CRUDITES
VEGETABLE SALAD

SHOW 187
POULET AUX NOIX
CHICKEN PECANDINE
HARICOTS VERTS CREOLE
CREOLE GREEN BEANS

SHOW 188
SUPREME DE VOLAILLE EN CROUTE
CHICKEN BAKED WITH MUSHROOM SAUCE IN FILO
SALADE D'EPINARDS
SPINACH SALAD

SHOW 189
RAGOUT D'ECREVESSE
CRAWFISH STEW
RIZ BOUILLI
BOILED RICE
SALADE DES HARICOTS VERTS
MARINATED GREEN BEAN SALAD

SHOW 190
ESCALOPES DE DINDE AU FOUR
BAKED TURKEY SCALLOPS
SOUPE PORTUGAISE
CABBAGE AND POTATO SOUP

SHOW 191
ESCALOPES DE PORC GRATINEES
PORK AND MUSHROOMS GRATIN
VELOUTE D'OIGNON
CREAM OF ONION SOUP

SHOW 192
HACHIS PARMENTIER
BEEF AND POTATOES AU GRATIN
VELOUTE NANTAIS
CREAM OF SHRIMP SOUP NANTAIS

SHOW 193
SPAGHETTI CARUSO
SPAGHETTI WITH CHICKEN LIVERS
INSALATA MISTA
MIXED ITALIAN SALAD

SHOW 194
CREVETTES FRITS A LA SAUCE BIERE
SHRIMP IN BEER BATTER
SALADE DE CHAMPIGNONS ITALIENNE
ITALIAN MUSHROOM SALAD

SHOW 195
CRABE IMPERIAL
CRAB IMPERIAL
SALADE D'EPINARDS BLANCHIS
WILTED SPINACH SALAD

SHOW 196
BEIGNETS DE JAMBON
HAM AND CHEESE FRITTERS
SALAD BEATRICE
GREEN BEAN AND TOMATO SALAD

SHOW 197
OEUFS A L'ALSACIENNE
EGGS AND SAUERKRAUT GRATINEE
TOMATES PROVENCALE
COUNTRY STYLE TOMATOES

SHOW 198
POULET MARINE FRIT
MARINATED FRIED CHICKEN
POMMES DE TERRE GRATINEES
POTATOES GRATIN

SHOW 199
CROUSTADES AUX ANCHOIS
POACHED EGGS IN BREAD CASES
CHAMPIGNONS SAUTEES
SAUTEED MUSHROOMS

SHOW 200
CELEBRATION - 200IEME PROGRAM
CELEBRATION - 200TH SHOW
HORS D'OEUVRESVARIES
VARIOUS APPETIZERS
CHAMPAGNE
CHAMPAGNE

Index of Recipes

The recipes in volume I are included in this index. Their titles ae printed in italics and (I) preceeds the page number. The recipes for volume II are printed in regular type and do not have a volume indication.

INDEX TO RECIPES

GRAPE LEAVES

GARLIC

GREEN BEANS

GREEN PEAS

HAM

SAUSAGE

SCALLOPS

SHRIMP

SOUP

SPINACH